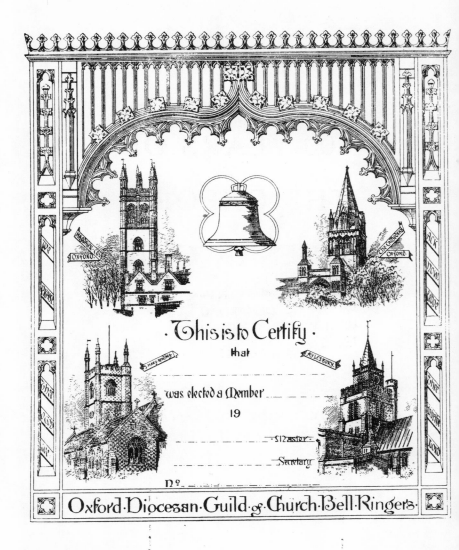

This is to Certify

that

was elected a Member

19

Master

Secretary

No.

Oxford·Diocesan·Guild·of·Church·Bell·Ringers·

100 YEARS OF

THE OXFORD

DIOCESAN GUILD

by

William Butler

THE OXFORD DIOCESAN GUILD
7 THE WAVERLEYS, THATCHAM, BERKS.

Published by
The Oxford Diocesan Guild
7 The Waverleys, Thatcham, Berks.

First published November 1981

c   William Butler

ISBN 0 9507832 O X

Printed by
Newbury Weekly News (Printers) Ltd.,
34 Northbrook Street, Newbury, Berks.

CONTENTS

LIST OF PLATES

PREFACE

"Watch the Oxford Guild! If it is flourishing then all is well with the Exercise; if it is in the doldrums then bell ringing is generally on the decline."

The Ringing World

If any justification is needed for this book, it may be found in these opening words of the editorial article of 26th July 1946. The Oxford Diocesan Guild became one of the most important associations in the country within a few years of its formation, and has remained amongst the leaders ever since.

It ranks fourth largest in area, behind Yorkshire, Lincolnshire and Devon. The latter has about a dozen more towers within its bounds, but these are split between two associations. In one sphere the Guild has always been pre-eminent, and this is in the number of members who man its bells. Five years after its foundation it became the largest guild in the country, and it has remained so. These members have included some wonderful ringers, some extraordinary characters, and hundreds of ordinary men and women whose sole involvement is in Sunday Service ringing.

The bibliography gives a list of the books consulted in researching this work. The quantity of minute books generated by fifteen branches in one hundred years is enough to quail the heart of the most earnest historian! The people who have aided me in compiling this history are too numerous to mention, although I give them my grateful thanks. The photographs have been supplied from many sources, and I must thank G. Anslow, D. Moore, R. Goodwin and M. E. Dobson for their help in producing them.

Finally, I must thank my wife Jennifer for her patience and forbearance whilst I painfully plodded through the rough draft, and her skill in typing, revising and reading the proofs. Without her help the book would never have been completed!

October 1981   **WILLIAM BUTLER**

Chapter One

IN THE BEGINNING ...

*"This is an art that is peculiar to England, and England for
this reason is termed the Ringing Island."*
Sir John Hawkins.

England has always been celebrated for its bells. Many foreigners
noted in their diaries, while travelling in this country, the great ringing of
bells that could be heard from almost all the churches. Paul Hentzer, for
example, commented in his *Travels in England* (1598) that the English were
very fond of bells:

"so that in London it is common for a number of them that have got a
glass in their heads to go up in some belfry and ring the bells for hours
together, for the sake of exercise."

He could have been writing about any village in this country. For
centuries the bells had been part of the life of the parish, ringing out for all
the ecclesiastical ceremonies that took place throughout the day. Then
came the Reformation, and their use for services was curtailed; only one
was allowed to be tolled. All superstitious uses ceased; it was no longer
possible to ring the passing bell to ward off evil spirits, but a bell could be
rung to call men to pray for the dying.

The result of these restrictions was to make the ringing of bells a
secular matter. Bells rang out on civic occasions — to welcome the Royal
Family or the Lord of the Manor, or to call people together to announce a
victory on land or sea. They rang as much as before, but instead of ringing
for the work of God, they broadcast only men's earthly affairs.

At the same time, the art of ringing was developing. The quarter and
half wheel had given way to the three-quarter and full wheel, and it had
been discovered that an excellent sport and exercise could be enjoyed by
swinging a bell higher and higher until it rang full circle. It could even be
held at the point of balance. From then on it was not long before someone
found that two bells rung consecutively could be rung in reverse order, by
swinging the first a little higher than the second. So the art of call changes
evolved, and in the second quarter of the seventeenth century the sixes and
plain changes were being rung. It was a short step from this to change
ringing. Societies began to spring up, whose members all had a common
interest in the sport. Some flourished, while others passed swiftly away.
One of the survivors was the Oxford Society.

Trollope, in the *College Youths* tells us that the Inns of Court and the
two universities were the main centres instrumental in the growth of
ringing. We are indebted to Anthony Wood, the Oxford antiquary, for a
glimpse of ringing in Oxford at that time. In 1653 he learnt to ring at
Cassington, a village halfway between Oxford and Witney. He had gone
there to convalesce after an illness, and decided to take up a new hobby
when he heard the recently installed ring of six. On his return to Oxford, he
joined in with the Oxford Society and described ringing at Merton College
like this:

"The bells did not at all please the curious and critical hearer. However he plucked at them often with some of his fellow colleagues for recreation's sake."

He would have joined the ringing fraternity in Oxford too late to know such men as Thomas Joyce, the son of a Dorsetshire gentleman, who in 1641 became the Master of the College Youths after he came down from the University. Sir Richard Atkins was another who rang while he was up at Oxford; he became Sheriff of Buckingham in 1649, and was created a baronet at the Restoration.

Anthony Wood could have known people like Sir John Brereton, the younger brother of Lord Brereton, one of the founders of the College Youths. Francis Withins, who was born at Eltham in 1634, also learnt to ring while he was at Oxford. He went on to become a lawyer and achieved fame, or notoriety, as one of the five judges presiding at the Bloody Assize in 1685. Other ringers at Oxford during this period were Leonard Lichfield, the printer to the University of Oxford; John Dolben, the son of the Archbishop of Canterbury, and Joseph Holland, the warden of Merton College. Holland was evidently unpopular; when he was installed as Rector of East Hendred, Berks, the ringers rang the bells backwards, as a mark of their dislike!

Richard Duckworth was well-known too. He was a Leicestershire man who matriculated in Oxford in 1648, graduating with a B.A. in 1651 from New Inn Hall. He took holy orders and preached locally for some years. He was made a Fellow of Brasenose College, and became Rector of Steeple Aston in 1679. Thirteen years later he returned to Oxford as principal of St. Alban Hall. He died on 19th July 1706, and his memorial is on the south wall of the chancel of Steeple Aston church.

There is evidence that he was instituted as Rector of Hartest, Suffolk in 1660. This is a small village some six and a half miles north west of Lavenham, and about thirty miles from Cambridge. It has always been assumed that Duckworth met Fabian Stedman at Cambridge, where Stedman probably worked as a printer for the University Press. It is conceivable, however, that they met in Oxford, where a branch of the Stedman family lived. It is also significant that, apart from London, the only other places to have printing works were the university towns of Oxford and Cambridge.

Wherever they met, they soon discovered their mutual passionate interest in ringing and so they collaborated in producing the first book on change ringing. Previous writers have suggested that Stedman provided the technical content, and Duckworth the literary skill. Duckworth was, according to his contemporaries, a talented ringer, so Stedman may have been involved only in the technicalities of arranging for the book to be printed. It was far more difficult to get a book printed then, for each one had to be licensed. Stedman would have been au fait with all the procedures for accomplishing this and the title page shows he was the publisher; Roger L'Estrange issued the licence in 1667.

For many years it was thought that Stedman was the author, yet

Wood's diary is quite clear that "he (Duckworth) hath written *Tintinnalogia, or the Art of ringing.*"

Tintinnalogia was reprinted in 1671 and six years later Stedman brought out a new book of his own called *Campanalogia*. He gathered information from all the centres of ringing he could contact and his book shows fifty-three methods that were being rung by the societies in London; seventeen were contributed by Samuel Scattergood from Cambridge, two from Nottingham, one from Reading and fifteen from Oxford. Among these were: Oxford Single, Double, and Treble Bob, Halliwell, Fortune, Paradox, Medley, My Lord, Camelion, and others with similar exotic names.

Ringers in other parts of the country became aware of the fascination of change ringing through the distribution of *Campanalogia,* and the closing years of the seventeenth century saw the art firmly established in at least half a dozen centres. In this, Oxford, and its ringers, had played an important part.

Chapter Two

RINGING IN THE DIOCESE PRIOR TO 1881

Change ringing was firmly established in Oxford in the seventeenth century, and during the next hundred and fifty years it was kept alive by the men who joined the Oxford Society. Their peal book records that from their first in 1734 they range ninety peals up to the foundation of the Guild. This is not a complete record for it is known that more peals were rung, but not entered. A history of the Society will prove of great value in determining how many people were involved; Philip Walker is undertaking this research.

The introduction of change ringing into a tower generally stimulated a desire for the bells to be augmented. During 1655, Michael Darbie, an itinerant founder, recast the six bells of New College, Oxford, into a new ring of eight — the first time a founder is known to have cast a complete octave of bells. Two years later he carried out a similar job for Merton College. Anthony Wood was disgusted with these bells, and the College cannot have been satisfied, for they engaged Christopher Hodson to recast them again in 1680. Merton College has the oldest complete ring of eight bells cast by one founder.

Hodson was in Oxford primarily to add four trebles to Christ Church to make it one of the first rings of ten — an ambitious project for, at that time, founders had not mastered the art of casting small bells that would not be overpowered by the larger bells of the ring. Samuel Smith had the same problems when he cast the four trebles for York Minster in 1681. In 1712 Magdalen College were augmented to eight and New College to ten. A move to have St. Mary the Virgin augmented to either eight or ten was made in 1724, but nothing ever came of it.

With the choice of two tens and an eight, it was hardly surprising that the College Youths selected Oxford for their excursion in 1733. Peals were not common achievements; the first was rung only in 1715, and subsequent attempts had been successful in thirteen places besides London and Norwich.

In the spring of 1733 fifteen members of the College Youths walked the fifty-five miles from London, and after resting for a day, they went for a peal at Christ Church. Their ringing was excellent, but the maintenance of the bells had been neglected; after two and a quarter hours, the tenor dropped out of its bearings. Nothing daunted, they set out for New College the following day, and had the misfortune to break three ropes during the first forty-five minutes ringing. Rather annoyed, they had to spend the rest of the day splicing ropes! Then they went for the peal again; the inevitable rope break came after two hours' ringing. Despite their lack of success in scoring peals, they had enjoyed their holiday and were not downcast as they walked back to London.

Spurred on by the quality of the Londoners' ringing, the Oxford Society practised hard, and rang the first peal to be accomplished in the diocese of Oxford — Grandsire Caters at New College — on 1st January 1734. Later that year they rang a further peal of 6,876 changes of Grandsire Caters in four hours. Further details of their activities are beyond the scope of this book; suffice it to say that they were the mainstay of change ringing in this part of the Diocese.

Elsewhere in Oxfordshire there was little activity. In 1709 Great Tew were recast into a pleasant eight by Abraham Rudhall, and nine years later Henry Bagley III did similar work at Kirtlington. He also added the two trebles at Burford in 1733. Probably the next augmentation to eight was at Witney in 1765. Great Milton followed in 1771 and ten years later Thomas Janaway, of Chelsea, cast a new eight for Benson.

Other founders obtaining work in the county included Robert Wells of Aldbourne, who supplied the two new trebles at Woodstock, paid for by the Marquis of Blandford in 1785. In 1789 John Briant of Hertford provided Adderbury with a new ring of eight. Early in the next century St. Ebbe's, Oxford were augmented to eight, when two trebles were donated, one by Mr Baker, a plumber, and the other by Mr. Scarsbrook, a collar-maker. The bells only rang for forty years, for they were sold in 1843, reducing the ring to a six again.

In the north of the county the old church at Banbury had a Bagley ring of six. The locals decided to build a new church in 1793, and a great deal of effort went into demolishing the old one. It proved so obstinate, that they resorted to blowing it up with gun-powder! When the new church was finished the old bells were augmented by two bells cast by John Briant, and installed in 1820.

At the opposite end of the county was Henley, right on the banks of the Thames. All the bells there were recast into a new ring of eight by Thomas Mears in 1813. Twelve years later John Rudhall of Gloucester supplied a brand new ring for Chipping Norton to go in their recently completed tower. An advertisement in *The Gloucester Journal* for 1st May

1826 indicated the churchwardens' willingness to give three prizes, of five pounds, three pounds and two pounds for the best three sets of changes rung at the opening of the bells.

In 1870 Bicester bells were augmented by the addition of a treble and a tenor, supplied by Mears and Stainbank. Three years earlier the same firm had cast two trebles for Dorchester Abbey, a six since 1651, the tenor of which was an ancient bell, recognised as such in Anthony Wood's time.

Probably the last ring of eight cast before the formation of the Guild was for Thame, which was supplied by Mears and Stainbank in 1876.

Change ringing was slow to take hold in the rural county of Buckingham. The first ring of eight was cast by James Bartlett of Whitechapel from the old five bells at Denham in 1683. Richard Phelps, one of his successors, was paid £140 for recasting the six at High Wycombe into an eight. Seven years later Abraham Rudhall replaced the five at Bletchley with one of his stock rings of eight, casting the tenor only to show the name of the donor of the ring. He was Browne Willis, who lived at Whaddon a few miles away and was very interested in bells. Born in 1682, he learnt to ring while he was up at Oxford, and later became friendly with Thomas Hearne, the Oxford historian.

Fig. 1. Browne Willis.

Thomas Hearne knew a great deal about bells and ringing; his father and uncle were ringers at Shottesbrooke, Berkshire, and his diaries give a fascinating picture of ringing at that time. Browne Willis wrote a history of Buckinghamshire, which is contained in 110 closely written volumes, preserved in the Bodleian Library. In this work he gives the number of bells in each church and Cocks includes extracts from it in his *Church Bells of Buckinghamshire.*

Over thirty years were to elapse before the next large-scale work was carried out. This was at Newport Pagnell, where Richard Phelps recast all the bells, making a very pleasant ring of eight.

The Union Scholars was a London based society, doing most of its ringing in the vicinity of St. Martins-in-the-Fields during the first half of the eighteenth century. Their furthest excursion into the country was in 1751, when they visited High Wycombe. Their records show that their thirtieth peal was on the 28th December 1751 at Chipping Wycombe, where John Holt called 5040 Plain Bob Triples. This was the first peal to be rung in Buckinghamshire.

The band at Buckingham were of a different disposition; they clung to their old rounds ringing, interspersed with bouts of drunken behaviour. Their habit of bringing their beer into the church and on to the balcony from which they rang aroused the wrath of many of the gentry, including Browne Willis. In 1737 he instigated a plan to increase the height of the tower so a new ringing chamber would be constructed "out" of church. This work was not undertaken until 1753, when the top of the tower was raised by twenty-four feet. For twenty-three years the ringers used this "secular" ringing room; then on 26th March 1776 the tower crashed to the ground — only minutes after the ringers had left! It was thought that the extra weight of the masonry added in 1753 had proved too much for the old piers, causing the collapse. The Buckingham ringers' bad habits had cost their church dearly. The damage was rectified, and Chapman and Mears supplied a new ring of eight in 1782. With a tenor of 27 cwts., they still form the heaviest octave in the county.

Further south the Long Crendon ringers were agitating to have their bells augmented. The five they had were bought from Nottley Abbey in 1539 on its dissolution. They were heavy; the tenor was reputed to be the largest bell in the county with a weight of 40 cwts. In 1768 these bells were taken to Whitechapel, where Lester and Pack cast a new ring of eight, with a tenor of nearly a ton. No details of ringing at that time survive, but in the nineteenth century, a band capable of quarter peals of Grandsire Triples emerged.

In the third quarter of the eighteenth century the bells of the present county town of Aylesbury were in a bad state. Of the six bells, the treble, fifth and tenor were cracked, and the remainder were in urgent need of the attentions of a bell hanger. On 30th March 1773 it was decided to put all the bells into the melting pot and have a new ring of eight, with a tenor of 22 cwts. Pack and Chapman cast them and a band of College Youths was invited from London to open them on 12th July. No peal is recorded, so either they did not have permission to go for one on this occasion, or an attempt was unsuccessful. Several weeks earlier what may have been the same band of College Youths were at Denham, where they rang 5,040 Plain Bob Major in three hours sixteen minutes, the second peal to be scored in the county.

The local band at High Wycombe were anxious to have their bells made up to ten — we do not know whether their change ringing skill merited such an augmentation or whether they wanted the prestige a ring of ten brought! In 1788 John Briant of Hertford added two trebles, creating the first ten in the county. On one of their country pilgrimages in 1792, the College Youths rang a peal of 5,111 Grandsire Caters in three hours forty-two minutes. One of the peal band, James Worster, may have been related to one of the locals, who had the same surname.

An interesting item about the Newport Pagnell ringers appeared in the *Northamptonshire Mercury* for 17th August 1793; all nine ringers signed a letter defending themselves against an allegation that they had rung the bells for the victory at Valenciennes only because they had been paid to do so. They waxed indignant and properly so, for it transpired that the letter accusing them was a hoax!

The next record of change ringing occurred in 1799 when a peal of Grandsire Triples was rung in three hours twelve minutes at Denham by the Society of Ringers from New Windsor.

The Aylesbury band had been making good progress and the advent of the new century prompted them to go for a peal. It was 12th November 1804, however, before they accomplished their aim, with 5,040 Grandsire Triples in three hours sixteen minutes.

Haddenham lay halfway between Great Milton and Aylesbury, with Long Crendon only a few miles away, so eight-bell bands were springing up all round. William Richmond, a Haddenham ringer, decided that his tower too should have eight bells, and agitated until sufficient money was raised to employ John Briant to recast the old five in 1809. Five years later Wooburn were augmented by adding two trebles, and in 1834 Marlow were made up to an eight by the addition of a treble and a tenor, and the flattening of the new fifth by a semi-tone.

Marlow was the venue for the next known record of change ringing in the county; on 5th June 1843, a band of College Youths, under the leadership of Thomas Tolladay, rang a peal of Grandsire Triples. J. R. Haworth, of whom more will be heard later, also stood in this peal. Thomas Tolladay, a boat builder by trade, rang originally in Windsor, but he moved away from the area about 1830 to further his ringing ambitions. At that time, he was one of the cleverest ringers in London, and he established the St. James Society as a leading company. After his success at Marlow, he went on to call another peal of Grandsire Triples at Wooburn. No other peals seem to have been rung in the county until after the formation of the East Berks and South Bucks Society in 1879.

During the seventeenth century ringing in Oxfordshire was concentrated almost exclusively in the city of Oxford. In contrast Berkshire had three centres, Windsor in the east, Newbury in the west and Reading in the middle.

Stedman's *Campanalogia* included only one method from Reading, called, naturally enough, Reading Doubles. It would not be recognised as a very good method today, for it had two separate blue lines and bells only transferred from one to the other at a bob! The Reading ringers, however, were very proud of it and it was even exported to Cambridge. With the greater variety of methods available to them, the Cambridge men were more critical, and by 1677 they produced a variation called "Reading Doubles the Cambridge way"!

As the foremost change ringing band in the county, the ringers of St.

Lawrence, Reading, were anxious to practise on higher numbers, and in 1662 they appealed to the parish to augment their five bells to eight; their request was successful and Henry Knight III cast them a complete octave that same year.

Twelve years earlier the ringers at Windsor Castle had persuaded the authorities to increase the number of bells in the Curfew Tower to eight, making the first ring of eight in the county. Unfortunately no record of any change ringing in Windsor at that time survives. We shall see later, though, how active the band was in the eighteenth century.

At the other end of the county the Newbury ringers were keen and in 1668 they invited the Reading Youths on a visit and entertained them royally. It is quite possible that, in return for their hospitality, they were instructed in the new art of change ringing; by 1680 they had induced the churchwardens to approach Henry Knight about replacing their old ring of six with a new eight, for which he charged £67. Any skill that the Newbury ringers acquired seemed to vanish quite quickly for no record of any change ringing exists until the last quarter of the nineteenth century. The bells were recast in 1803 into a new heavier ring by James Wells of Aldbourne.

There was clearly a good band of ringers at Hurst for many years; their name appears frequently during the eighteenth and nineteenth centuries in connection with striking contests. They remained quite content with their call changes and never ventured into the new fangled change ringing. In the seventeenth century they may have been one of the first bands to visit another tower; the records at Great Marlow show that the Hurst ringers were invited to try out the bells after they were rehung in 1640. The host churchwardens paid all expenses for the expedition, a round trip of about thirty miles, and the visitors had a thoroughly good time!

The first written record of change ringing in the county is to be found on a peal board at St. Lawrence's, Reading, proclaiming that the whole peal of Grandsire Triples, conducted by Henry Peaty, was rung in three hours and ten minutes on 8th July 1734. In 1740 he stood in a peal of Union Triples with three other members of the original band to christen the newly augmented eight at St. Mary's, Reading. William Strode and John Blagrave had paid £102 7s. 10d. to provide two treble bells, which Robert Catlin cast. He had succeeded to the foundry of Samuel Knight, who had moved from Reading to Holborn in 1709 when work in the area became scarce.

In 1742 the Reading Youths rang another peal of Grandsire Triples at St. Mary's, which they described as only the second peal of its kind. Presumably they were just referring to their own records for by then many such peals had been rung in different parts of the country.

Prior to 1740 Robert Catlin had rung a number of peals with the College Youths, and it seems likely that he sang the praises of St. Mary's Reading among London ringing circles, for in 1744 the College Youths visited Reading and scored the first peal of Major to be rung in the Diocese. This feat took place in three hours twenty-six minutes on 15th May; John

Trenell rang the tenor, an excellent performance, considering it had needed two men to ring it behind for the peal of Union Triples four years before. The peal was conducted by Benjamin Annable, their long-standing leading member.

On their country forays the College Youths often persuaded a church warden or some other dignitary to present a peal board recording their exploits, and the board for this peal was surmounted with a bell and their motto "Intactum sileo, percute dulce cano" (Untouched I am a silent thing, Strike me and I sweetly sing).

The Reading Youths decided to prove to themselves that they were not only the equals of the College Youths, but better men. For nine months they practised hard and on the morning of 3rd March 1745 they attempted a peal of 10,080 Bob Major. All went well for five hours fifty-nine minutes when the rope on the third parted; they had accomplished 8,176 changes. They were bitterly disappointed, especially the older men — Robert Booth who had rung in all the other peals and John Lucas who had sweated on the tenor for nearly six hours. Each time they went into the ringing room and saw the board recording the College Youths' success, they felt more and more aggrieved. They could hardly invite someone to give a board for a peal which had been lost! Eventually a brilliant solution was conceived; they would use the board already there . . . The College Youths' names were painted out and the details of the Reading men's glorious failure superimposed. The motto of that other Society was left at the top, however!

At the church of St. Lawrence, the bells were in a poor state; it was more than eighty years since Henry Knight had added two trebles to the old six, and the state of the seventeenth century gear prevented prolonged ringing. The skill and enthusiasm of the Reading Youths was on the ascendant; they decided to raise sufficient money to recast the eight and perhaps add two new trebles to make a ten. They set to work with a will and in 1748 Robert Catlin installed the new ring. Before the year was out they had achieved a peal of Grandsire Caters. After this flurry of activity the company seems to have lapsed into lethargy, not to rise to prominence again until the 1870s.

In 1711 the Windsor ringers were thrilled to be presented with a new ring of bells. A modern ring of eight, cast by Richard Phelps of Whitechapel, were installed in the parish church of St. John. All expenses were met by Samuel Masham, who had married Queen Anne's Court favourite, Abigail Hill, four years before.

It is a great pity that the first record book of the Windsor ringers has been lost. The existing volume dates from 1787 and refers to an earlier book. It is tantalising to speculate on what change ringing may have been accomplished in those distant days.

There is a board in the Curfew Tower recording a peal of Union Triples on 21st February 1748; it claims it was never performed in the tower before. But does that mean the peal or the method? One of the two men on the tenor was William Cock, a well-known local publican, who had been a witness in a controversy over bribery at the 1715 General Election.

He was a College Youth and may have been related to the ringing family of the same name at Great Marlow in the previous century.

Forty years later, the College Youths visited Windsor and rang a peal of Grandsire Triples at the Castle on 10th April 1787, conducted by James Worster; the seventh and tenor required the strength of two men each.

The established Society of Ringers of New Windsor remained active, although their next peal was not until 1798 when they scored Grandsire Triples at St. John's. It was not claimed as the first on the bells, so it is feasible that others may have been rung there and the records lost. In the following year they travelled to Denham for the peal mentioned earlier.

Ringing for money dominated the band after this period. They were employed by the Castle to ring for Royal birthdays and other ceremonial occasions, whilst the Mayor and Corporation paid them for ringing at St. John's for civic ceremonies. For example, during the 1820 General Election, they rang the bells three times daily — at 8.00 a.m. noon and 8.00 p.m. — for fifteen days in succession. This produced an income of £121 to be divided between the sixteen ringers involved. Of course, the money provoked arguments, and the ringers fell out, splitting into two bands. One rang at the Castle and the other at the parish church. Neither was strong enough alone for change ringing to survive and so the ringing returned to rounds and call changes for the next fifty years or so.

Several other towns augmented their bells to eight during the eighteenth century. The first was Wallingford in 1738, followed by Lambourn in 1742 and St. Helen's, Abingdon in 1762. There is no record of change ringing at these towers at that time. Robert Wells added two bells at East Hagbourne in 1770, and a local band successfully rang a peal later in the year.

In 1778 Pack and Chapman augmented Sonning to eight, and these bells provided the venue for a famous ringing contest five years later. The Farnham ringers, the Oxford Society and the College Youths competed for a silver cup, presented by a local landowner. It is surprising that the Reading and Windsor bands were not participating; perhaps their ringing was at a low ebb then. The College Youths won and the cup is one of their treasured possessions, brought out on ceremonial occasions.

The Reading Mercury contains many reports of the ringing contests which flourished along the Thames and Kennet valleys during the final part of the century. Cyril Wratten has compiled an excellent account of these, which was published in *The Ringing World* in 1978. In a typical match, for instance, at Wokingham in 1776 several teams competed for six hats. The account reports that "the Hurst Youths won in their usual style," whilst the Reading Youths were second, and teams from Mortimer and Binfield came third and fourth.

These events were a regular feature and one was reported in the *New Monthly Magazine* like this:

> "A ringing match took place at Hurst, Berkshire, for a silver cup and six beaver hats by six sets of ringers. The cup was won in great style by the Reading Youths and the hats by the Mortimer Youths. The ringing

in general was performed in the best manner and a great number of people attended."

In the first quarter of the nineteenth century a new centre arose in North Berkshire, when the Appleton Society was formed on 4th March 1818. They rang their first 720 on the bells about three years later, and their prowess continued to increase in the ensuing twenty years. In 1854 Alfred White, the founder of the famous bell-hanging business, opened a fund to augment the bells, and a new treble and a second-hand tenor were soon obtained. Their first peal of Grandsire Triples was accomplished within the year, and after that peals followed regularly, including Kent Treble Bob Major in 1859 and Stedman Triples in 1861. The Stedman was achieved after many fruitless attempts, the last was on the morning of the successful peal!

F. E. Robinson, then a partner in the Old Bank, Oxford, rang in this series of peals and was so pleased with them that he gave two trebles to make Appleton the second ring of ten in the county. In the same year a peal of Grandsire Caters was rung, to be followed a few months later by one of Stedman Caters. Much to the disappointment of the band the composition for the Stedman proved false. Since then peals have been rung regularly, including a number of long lengths. The first was 10,080 Grandsire Caters on 4th March 1871 in six hours twenty-one minutes.

London based bands visited Windsor in 1830 and 1850 to ring peals; the first, conducted by Thomas Tolladay, was for the St. James' Society and the second for the College Youths.

New rings of eight were installed by John Warner at St. Paul's Wokingham in 1864 and All Saints, Boyne Hill in 1868. In the same year Boyne Hill was destroyed by fire and the bells had to be recast. There is a story that when this second ring were being installed, the tackle broke, dropping one of the bells from high in the tower, through the hole in the stone-vaulted ceiling with inches to spare. It came to rest partially buried in the ground. With trepidation the bell hanger approached it and was amazed to find it unharmed!

The only other augmentation to eight before the formation of the Guild was at Faringdon in 1874, when Mears and Stainbank added two trebles.

By 1879 there was a move in the eastern part of the county to form an association of ringers, similar to those springing up in other parts of the country. Early that year the East Berks and South Bucks Society was set up, based initially on Boyne Hill and Farnham Royal. Later it expanded to take in most of the surrounding towers, although Slough remained for some time in the West Middlesex Association, which it had joined in 1874.

The ringers in the Sonning area watched the progress of the East Berks and South Bucks Society with interest and in 1880 they established the Sonning Deanery Society. Revds. Dolben Paul, H. C. Sturges and R. H. Hart-Davis, all practical ringers, gave their support to the new group. These two societies provided the model for the Oxford Diocesan Guild when it came into existence in 1881.

Chapter Three

FORMATION OF THE GUILD

"Ringers and singers are little home bringers"
18th century proverb

In the early part of Queen Victoria's reign about seventy per cent of the population were nominally members of the Church of England, which had separated from the Church of Rome as a consequence of Henry VIII's domestic problems. It retained an external resemblance to Roman Catholicism, although many people had a great fear of "Popery", imagining it would bring foreign political domination.

The Oxford Movement was born in 1833 when a small group of young High Church men struck out at clerical complacency. Although their motives were good, their activities caused a division into High Church and Low Church, neither of which was very tolerant of the other. They were, however, united in their desire to see reforms. Their supporters renovated churches with great zeal, ripping out old furniture and replacing it with new. They swept away the old barrel organs and fiddlers of the eighteenth century and installed new organs to lead the singing. The old bands of singers were replaced with a sedate, robed choir. To complete their work, the reformers turned their attention to the ringing chamber.

Here they met considerable opposition. Events of the previous centuries had secularised ringing. There was firm hostility, not only from those in the belfry, but also from the congregation, to whom ringing had become part of the English heritage.

The reputation of ringers throughout the country was generally poor. There were few centres of change ringing in the diocese and elsewhere the majority of bands performed only for the money they could earn, immediately squandering it in the alehouse when ringing was over. Conversion was necessary, and had to come. It is fortunate that it came from within the Exercise; had it been left to the ideologists, ringing would have followed the barrel organs and fiddlers into obscurity.

The movement for revision was spear-headed by men like Revd H. T. Ellacombe and Canon Woolmore Wigram. In *Practical Remarks on Ringers and Belfries* Ellacombe advocated introducing a new class of men into the ringing chamber, teaching them change ringing and regarding them as church workers. From here the idea of territorial and diocesan associations was to develop. These days it is difficult to realise how radical this scheme was, for the societies then were very small and parochial. For instance the College Youths had fewer than a hundred and fifty members during its first hundred years of existence. An average band consisted of less than a dozen men, and this was the extent of their involvement with other ringers.

The Oxford University Society, founded in 1874, had been diligent in recruiting undergraduates, who later on became some of the leaders of the new territorial associations and guilds. In the south of the diocese, the border town of Slough had been attracted into joining the West Middlesex Association, also formed in 1874. The East Berks and South Bucks Society was started in 1879, gathering about two dozen ringers from Boyne Hill and Farnham Royal. Finally there was the Sonning Deanery Society, dating from May 1880.

The initiative for the Sonning Deanery Society had come from a small group of clergy. At a local chapter meeting held on 23rd October, 1879, they formed a committee for "the incorporation of the bell ringers of the deanery into a society for the encouragement of change ringing." The three committee members who were most energetic in their pursuit of its objects were Dolben Paul, R. H. Hart-Davis and H. C. Sturges, who wrote a letter to *The Reading Mercury* published on 26th February 1880:

"Sir,

May I ask you to allow me a short space in your column to make known to your readers the foundation of a society, which has been lately formed in the neighbourhood of Reading, for the encouragement of the beautiful science of change ringing, and the cultivation of order, moral tone and reverence in our belfries? In a book which has lately been published, called *'A Guide to the Steeples of England,"* I notice that the churches of Reading and the neighbourhood are, for the most part, conspicuous by their absence. On asking the author of that book for the reason for this, I am told that Berkshire, though by no means deficient in fine bells, is yet singularly behind the other counties in its possession of real change ringers. It is in the endeavour to remove this reproach from our county that an Association has been formed under the presidency of John Walter Esq., MP of Bearwood, and a committee of clergymen, which has the cultivation of this science immediately in view. The Association at present embraces the churches of Wokingham (All Saints and St. Paul's), Arborfield, Hurst, Sonning and Wargrave. Already some gentlemen living in these parishes have become honorary members of the Society, and others are earnestly invited to do the same, if only to forward the object it has in view with their subscriptions. Any one within the deanery whose parish is not fortunate enough to possess a ring of bells, but who is capable of taking his bell through what is termed a plain course of Grandsire Doubles, is eligible to become a performing member of the Society on a small yearly payment. Many persons are not aware of the vast difference which exists between what is called "round ringing" and "change ringing." (Then followed an explanation of these terms). The science itself is of such a fascinating kind when once learnt, that a country squire who is a great rider to hounds and a keen sportsman, declared at a Church Congress not long since, that working his bell through all the intricacies of a peal of 5,040 changes in 2 hrs. and 40 mins. had given him far greater excitement and interest than he ever obtained in his best run or in his hottest corner at the cover-side. It is indeed a standing disgrace to our church that so little notice has hitherto been taken of the grand old bells which have been hung in our belfries, often at a cost of over a thousand pounds. Who would have supposed that our parishioners could so long have endured that six or eight rich musical notes, should for years have been struck in the scale which a child first uses on learning the piano? All lovers of church bells may now hope that a better state of things is in store for us. We understand that a similar Association has been formed to embrace the churches of East Berks and South Bucks, and we hope very soon to hear that Reading itself has formed a society for the same purpose.

Herbert C. Sturges (one of the Committee)

This gives some idea of the general state of ringing in the diocese. Apart from Oxford, Appleton and a few towers in the Maidenhead area, little change ringing took place. The time was right for a clean sweep and the enthusiasts were there to set it in motion.

The Sonning Deanery Society prospered and its initiators thought the climate right to expand their idea. Their senior member, Revd. Dolben Paul, took action; On 8th October, 1880 he read a paper to the Diocesan Conference, meeting in Oxford. He asked permission to form a Diocesan Guild of Ringers, opening his speech with these words:

"I appear before this conference today as the mouthpiece and representative of the Society of Change Ringers in my own Deanery of Sonning at whose request I have undertaken to bring this subject before you. That Society, embracing all the churches in the deanery which have a peal of bells, has been established just a year and has met with considerable support in the neighbourhood. The rules and list of subscribers I have by me. The Maidenhead Deanery has also started a similar society, but there seems to be a feeling among the members of each that it would be a great advantage to enlarge our area and to form a Diocesan Society at which all others could be affiliated. Such a society has already been established in the Diocese of Winchester and I hope to show to the satisfaction of this conference that it is a sensible course for this diocese also to adopt."

He went on to say that while almost every other branch of church work had been thoroughly overhauled and improved, the control of the bells had often been left in the hands of indifferent characters, usually recruited from the public houses. A Society of Change Ringers, such as he envisaged, would recruit a better class of men and ensure their recognition as church officers. He used the word "change" rather than "round" ringers advisedly, thinking that by making the distinction, a more skilful and intelligent class would be introduced into the belfries; choirs had been improved in a similar way when a higher standard of music was encouraged. He suggested that ringers would meet together annually, with perhaps two or three hours' ringing. Following this, there could be a talk under the presidency of some well-known layman or cleric of the diocese. He was sure that such a society could assist in framing rules for parochial associations to help forward the movement for better belfry management. In his conclusion, he sought the formation of a committee to set up the association.

The motion was seconded by Sir John Conroy, Bt., and was carried unanimously. The members of the conference wisely decided that they were not qualified to form the committee and asked for an open meeting to be held.

A few weeks later, *Church Bells,* at that time the only newspaper devoting a regular weekly column to ringing, contained an important announcement. A public meeting would be held at Reading on Saturday, 13th November and all ringers living in the diocese were invited to attend. It promised an exhibition of change ringing under Revd. F. E. Robinson's conductorship, with a shilling tea to follow!

The *Berkshire Chronicle* and *Church Bells* were enthusiastic about the ringing. The proceedings were opened at St. Mary's with 504 Grandsire Triples, rung by a picked band, consisting of J. E. A. Troyte, Master of the Oxford University Society, J. R. Haworth, G. Mash and E. Horrex of the College Youths, G. Holifield, F. White and T. Bennett of Appleton and Revd. F. E. Robinson from Drayton. This touch and those of Stedman and Grandsire that followed "afforded a treat to the ringers of the neighbourhood such as they have seldom, if ever, enjoyed before." Meanwhile at St. Giles, the ringers of the area rang the bells with "great spirit!"

About a hundred people, including leading ringers from the district, were present at the meeting which took place after the shilling tea. Nearly twenty per cent were members of the clergy who were all anxious to see this new instrument of belfry reform off to a good start. Many of them had more than a nodding acquaintance with ringing, for they had learnt to ring, either in their youth or during their time at Oxford or Cambridge.

Sir John Conroy formally opened the meeting and then Dolben Paul proposed that a Diocesan Guild of Church Bell Ringers be formed. This was seconded by the Vicar of St. Giles, Reading and was carried unanimously. A second resolution was passed to create a committee and Revd. F. E. Robinson arose, armed with a ready prepared list of committee members, who were promptly elected. The meeting concluded after a discussion on the terms of membership. There had certainly been some good staff work! The proposers and seconders were all obviously well-briefed.

Who were the members of this committee? Fundamentally it was soundly balanced, with seven clergymen and seven well-known ringers. Revd. F. E. Robinson, a College Youth, was an experienced ringer and conductor, although not then the acknowledged expert he would become. Revd. Dolben Paul, Rector of Bearwood, had far less practical knowledge of bells and ringing, but he did possess considerable drive and organising ability. Revd. H. C. Sturges, from Wargrave, was also a College Youth. He worked hard teaching his local band, and by dint of practising three times a week he was able to get them all through a 120 of Bob Doubles in six months; there is no record that he rang any peals, though. Revd. R. H. Hart-Davis was Vicar of Dunsden, and his practical ringing never progressed beyond the bell-handling stage. Like Dolben Paul, his ability lay in administration. Revd. S. F. Marshall and Revd. A. Drummond were founder members of the East Berks and South Bucks Society, and so obvious choices to serve on the committee. The last clerical member was Revd. H. Barter, Vicar of Shipton-under-Wychwood, and it seems likely that he had some ringing experience.

The lay members were better qualified. Capt. J. E. Ackland Troyte was the brother of the squire of Huntsham, Devon, who had written *Change Ringing*. John Troyte wrote *The Change Ringer's Guide to the Steeples of England* and was Master of the Oxford University Society. Charles Hounslow, from Oxford, was regarded by F. E. Robinson as one of his oldest ringing friends, and was known as "the grand old man of ringing" in the city. William Newell was held in similar regard by the Reading ringers, for he had worked hard for many years to establish a change ringing band in the town. J. J. Parker was aged about twenty-eight at this time and his enthusiasm for ringing and his skill as a composer were already evident. Edwin Rogers, from Boyne Hill, was the patriarch of ringing in the East Berks and South Bucks Society; he had persuaded the Farnham Royal ringers to take up change ringing, which led to the formation of the Society. The final man was R. E. Fiske, son of the Vicar of Northleigh, Oxon.

The committee held two meetings before the end of the year; Messrs Fiske, Parker, Hounslow and White did not attend either of them. Dolben Paul was elected secretary and treasurer, and also chaired the meetings. The main topic for discussion was a set of draft rules. When these were ready, copies were sent to all the county newspapers, together with a notice of an inaugural general meeting to be held in Oxford on 17th January, 1881.

The *Oxford University Herald* gives an account of this meeting, held in the rooms of the Churchmen's Institute, Broad Street with the Archdeacon of Berkshire in the chair. It is not clear how many people were present, but it seems likely that there were considerably fewer than at the first meeting at Reading. Some minor alterations were made to the draft rules, and then F. E. Robinson was elected Master and Dolben Paul Secretary and Treasurer. They were appointed till the first Annual General Meeting, which was scheduled for June, July or August. A committee was elected with six honorary members and six ringing members. From the original committee Messrs Hart-Davis, Fiske, Parker and Troyte stood down and their places were taken by Revd. H. A. Harvey, Revd. H. Davies, J. Field and R. Smith.

With this meeting, the Guild was formally established, albeit only in name.

Chapter Four

THE FIRST YEAR

The Guild had a name, officers and a committee, but not much else. It was for these men to put into practice the objects laid down in the second of the adopted set of rules: "to recognise the true position of ringers as church officers; to cultivate the art of change ringing and to promote belfry reform where needed." First, the Guild had to make ringers throughout the diocese aware of its existence. The committee decided that the best way of tackling this was to write to all thirty-one rural deans, explaining the objects of the Guild and encouraging them to persuade their chapters to form a local branch. Dolben Paul coped with this task, sending also copies of the rules which he had printed locally.

During the next seven weeks Dolben Paul wrote more than a hundred and twenty letters to incumbents in various parts of the diocese, seeking help in setting up branches. Wealthy and influential people who lived in the area were asked to give their support by becoming honorary or life members. It is interesting to note that life membership was originally intended as an additional class of honorary membership, and not for ringers at all! Some of those who responded to this request were: Rt. Hon. Sir John Mowbray, MP for the University of Oxford; T. O. Wethered, the brewer from Marlow; W. H. Smith, who was building up his chain of bookshops; Col. Sir Robert Lloyd-Lindsay, awarded the VC at the Battle of Alma, and Tory MP for Berkshire for thirty years; John Walter from Bearwood, whose grandfather had founded *The Times,* and of which he was the current editor, as well as serving as Liberal MP for Berkshire. Among the many others were William Mount, Sir Paul Hunter and Lady Wickens.

Offers of help in establishing local branches were soon forthcoming; Revd. J. Blomfield from Bicester was very anxious to start and requested enough copies of the rules to cover all his local towers. Several of the senior ringers at Oxford were keen to begin one in the city and William Newell hoped to do the same in Reading.

The honour of being the first new branch went to Oxford, when a meeting was held on Tuesday, 26th April, 1881 in St. Peter-in-the-East Schoolroom. Charles Hounslow was elected the first chairman and David Francombe secretary and treasurer. Hounslow and Joseph Field were appointed instructors to the fledgling branch, which consisted of only two towers, St. Peter-in-the-East and St. Mary Magdalen. The Holywell ringers attended the meeting but couldn't decide whether or not to join. They adjourned for a private conclave, and eventually opted out!

To join, the members of a band had to be proposed by their incumbent. Then their names went forward to the committee, where they were elected if they were vouched for by a competent ringer. The old band from Wantage, whose names were sent in by their Vicar, Rev. T. Houblon, were the first to be elected like this.

This occurred at the first committee meeting. Then Dolben Paul announced that more than £52 had been subscribed to the funds already. At the end of the discussion on how to spend this money it was agreed that certificates should be printed and one presented to each member after his election. The design was left in the Master's hands and it is possible that he engraved it as well as deciding on its form, for he certainly had the necessary skills.

Fifteen weeks after the Guild's inaugural meeting the membership was: life members 18, honorary members 62 and change ringing members 65. The latter were split evenly between those in the Sonning Deanery, the East Berks and South Bucks branch, and those not affiliated to a branch. There do not appear to have been any members from the new Oxford City Branch.

In the weeks that followed, Dolben Paul was extremely busy, writing a further hundred and twenty-five letters to ringers and clergy around the diocese, urging the formation of branches. Twelve rural deans promised to do their best but in the end only the rural dean from Newbury proved of positive help. He corresponded with William Newell, spurring him on to get the Reading branch organised, and he enlisted the assistance of the clergy in the town. Eventually a meeting was arranged for 5th July.

Besides this work, there were all the arrangements for the Annual General Meeting to make. Dolben Paul asked the various railway companies for cheap fares to be made available for members going to the meeting. He engaged the caterers, booked up all the towers for ringing, and finally sent out a copy of the printed programme to each member, enclosing a free dinner ticket. He probably heaved a sigh of relieved exhaustion when the last of the envelopes dropped into the post box!

Members from some of the Reading towers met on Tuesday, 5th July in St. Mary's School and decided to form a Reading branch. Revd. N. T. Garry, Vicar of St. Mary's, was elected the first chairman, William Newell was secretary and C. Stephens treasurer. Four towers joined; they were the three from Reading itself and Caversham. The Guild now had four branches attached to the parent body, for the Sonning Deanery Society had transferred its allegiance on 26th February and the East Berks and South Bucks Society followed suit soon afterwards.

This is a good time to consider what kind of men the officers of the guild were.

Dolben Paul was born in 1833, the second son of Samuel Woodfield Paul, Vicar of Finedon, Northants. His mother was a member of the Dolben family who owned Finedon Hall at that time. He matriculated from Westminster School in 1850, and followed five generations of his family in reading for a degree at Christ Church, Oxford.

During his boyhood at Finedon he had learned to ring and he was very proud that, apart from his father, there had been ringers in his family since the innovation of change ringing. A portrait of one of his ancestors, John Dolben, hangs in Christ Church Dining Hall today; under Charles II he was Dean of Westminster, ultimately becoming Archbishop of York.

Dolben Paul was ordained in 1856 and made a priest in the next year. After various curacies he was inducted Rector of Bearwood, Wokingham, in 1868, where he remained for the next twenty-three years. Although not an accomplished ringer himself, he was passionately fond of the Art, and he did his best to advance the cause of ringers. There is no doubt that his work set the Guild upon its firm foundations.

Francis Edward Robinson was born in the same year as Dolben Paul in Begbroke, Oxon. From Winchester, he went up to Exeter College, Oxford, graduating with a fourth class honours degree in 1853. From then till 1867 he worked in the Old Bank, Oxford, first as a clerk and later as a partner.

He learned to handle a bell while he was an undergraduate, but was not introduced to change ringing until he visited Appleton in 1859. He was taught by Alfred White and his sons, Henry and Frederick, and soon achieved his first peal that same year. His second peal was Kent Treble Bob Major, after which he began a long series of practice attempts for his first of Stedman. He accomplished this 1861 and was so delighted that he gave two tenors to Appleton at a cost of £254. Before his entry into the Church in 1868, he rang several more peals, including a false one of Stedman Caters. After his ordination, he abandoned ringing for four years, apart from one peal at Bethnal Green. He was curate at Tubney and lived at Appleton Vicarage; the disreputable conduct of some of the ringers accounted for his absence from the tower.

At last the situation improved and he resumed peal ringing in 1873. When Lord Wantage presented him to the living at Drayton, Berks, five years later, he had scored eighteen peals. To fulfill his ambition to be the first cleric to ring a peal on the bells of his own parish church, he gave a treble and tenor to augment the existing six at Drayton and went on to realise his dream. Before the formation of the Guild he rang another seven peals; he was a competent conductor and one of a rare breed then, for he had called peals of both Stedman Triples and Caters. He was obviously the man for the job of Master.

The first annual meeting held at Reading on Wednesday, 20th July, 1881 attracted a large number of ringers and clergy and the secretary regarded it as "a very successful gathering." The local press were invited to cover the meeting and *The Reading Mercury* printed a long and glowing account of the proceedings. There was a service at eleven o'clock at St. Mary's, where the address was given by the Very Revd. Purey-Cust, Dean of York, who had been the local incumbent some years earlier. His sermon was "long and deeply interesting." Indeed it must have been, for the precis published by the paper ran to more than two thousand words!

He dwelt upon the early superstitious uses of bells and the profanities to which they had been subjected during the eighteenth century. The purpose of the Guild was to cleanse the belfries of all abuses, and so make them a recognised part of the church. The bells themselves were capable of highly scientific, musical and religious treatment, and the clergy desired to see them used in that way.

The Foresters' Hall, Reading was the scene of great activity when one hundred and thirty-four people sat down to dinner. Members attended from nineteen towers; St. Mary, St. Lawrence and St. Giles, Reading; All Saints and St. Paul's Wokingham; Englefield, Sonning, Caversham, Sandhurst, Milton, Boyne Hill, Farnham Royal, Wargrave, Hurst, Arborfield, Wantage, St. Mary Magdalene, St. Thomas and St. Peter-in-the-East, Oxford.

During the speeches the Master rose for the first of very many occasions on which he addressed the Guild. In replying to the toast of "Prosperity to the Guild," he demonstrated his forceful personality and his strong and uncompromising attitude to the excesses that had occurred in belfries in the past. He admitted that the clergy deserved the lion's share of the blame, but said that they must seize the opportunity available to them to improve matters.

The secretary delivered his report, and, almost as an afterthought, the officers were elected for a further year. William Newell's handbell band entertained the company before it dispersed for an afternoon's ringing. The gathering ended after tea was consumed.

The summer saw little of consequence happening; Dolben Paul offered to send a Guild band to re-open Hughenden bells after re-hanging, but this suggestion was politely rejected by the Vicar. In September there were problems in the Oxford branch when an argument arose among the members probably over damage caused at Christ Church during a tower practice. Paul wrote many letters to the principal ringers and asked Revd. T. Chamberlain to intercede with the members for the good of the new branch, all to no avail. Field and Francombe visited him on 6th October, declaring that the branch wished to merge with the general Guild. They handed over the branch funds of six shillings and sixpence. The branch had existed for one hundred and sixty-three days.

On the whole the clergy of the diocese were in favour of the formation of branches. Revd. A. H. E. de Romsetin, rural dean of Woodstock, was much taken with the idea, suggesting setting one up in his deanery with Revd. F. Burra as secretary. The Vicar of Newbury, Revd. E. I. Gardiner, made enquiries for he had a number of young men interested in becoming members as well as his old band. Revd. H. Sturges was dispatched to Newbury to see if they qualified for change ringing membership. Finally Revd. C. H. Travers, rural dean of Bradfield, proposed that Revd. J. B. Burne should be secretary of a Bradfield branch.

Some of the change ringing members from Oxford decided it was time the first peal should be scored for the Guild so they approached Charlie Hounslow, asking him to call a peal on 26th November. This placed him in a predicament for he was supposed to be at the Guild Committee meeting in Reading on that day. The desire to ring overcame the chore of going to the meeting and he duly called Holt's Ten-Part at Kirtlington, Oxford.

The band were all Oxford ringers: Sam Buckle, on the treble, and James Washbrook, on the sixth, rang at St. Thomas; Charlie Hounslow, from St. Peter-in-the-East, called the peal from the fifth. The remaining five were members of the Oxford University Society, and had been officers at some time or another. A. B. Perceval rang the second, F. A. H. du Boulay rang the third, C. C. Child the fourth, G. F. Coleridge the seventh and H. F. Hastings the tenor. G. F. Coleridge was to become one of the Guild's Masters later in life.

At the meeting that Charlie Hounslow avoided, the rest of the committee were deciding how to speed up the election of new members. It was a cumbersome business; each man had to be vouched for by his parish priest, who confirmed he was of good character befitting a member of the Guild. His change ringing ability was assessed by a reputable member who endorsed the incumbent's report. The committee then considered the application; not everyone who applied was admitted. A. Fox of St. Peter-in-the-East Oxford applied unsuccessfully several times. Although he qualified as a change ringer, his vicar, Revd. Scott Mylne, would not give him a good character reference! Charles Doe, a Sandhurst ringer, had his membership withdrawn because he returned home drunk from a branch practice at Arborfield.

Athough the committee were unable to arrive at any conclusion, one good suggestion was made, that new members should be admitted on the recommendation of a Guild instructor. The matter was referred to a special meeting of the Guild, to be held in the Spring. The only other matter of importance to be discussed was the proposal to compile a book containing the names of all the members, with details of their towers and the weight of the bells, etc. They were quite impressed by one of these recently produced by the Norwich Diocesan Association. Nowadays the Annual Report is commonplace; a hundred years ago it was an entirely new venture and very few had been printed.

As the year drew to a close, the second peal was rung. On Boxing Day, a band from Oxford, with Joseph Field as conductor, rang Holt's Ten-Part at St. Paul's Wokingham. All the band were city ringers, and two of them were attempting their first peal. Dolben Paul had arranged the visit with David Francombe, and ten ringers turned up! After the peal they all met the Wokingham ringers and dined at the Rose Hotel. The Guild footed the bill, paying out one pound ten shillings, or five times the subscriptions contributed by the defunct city branch!

Chapter Five

EXPANSION

"Enlarging its borders, lengthening its cords, and strengthening its stakes."

1882 Annual Report

At the start of 1882 there were twenty-two towers affiliated to the Guild, with one hundred and ninety ringers spread amongst them. A further one hundred and twenty-three people had been induced to join as honorary or life members. In one way the latter were more essential than the ringing members; they added prestige, financial strength and, above all, respectability. By using their subscriptions, the Committee were able to defray the costs of tuition, free lunches and the other expenses that occurred during the year.

The ringing members were split into two classes. Change ringing members had to be able to hunt a bell through 120 changes, either on tower or handbells. Probationary members could be admitted on the recommendation of their incumbent. Of the hundred and ninety ringing members, eighty-two were probationers, i.e. only able to ring rounds or call-changes. They received exactly the same treatment as full members, with the exception that they could not serve on the management committee.

The year opened with the Guild's third peal. Revd. F. E. Robinson brought seven of the Appleton ringers to Drayton where he conducted the first of Stedman Triples for the Guild. Meanwhile other members of the Committee were working hard, recruiting. Revd. H. G. Sturges was able to report the successful launching of a new branch in the Newbury area; he had enrolled twenty-two members, all from Newbury tower. One of the band, W. A. Ranshaw, was co-erced into becoming the first secretary and one of his initial jobs was buying a new set of handbells. He acquired a secondhand set, which were not considered good enough, so a brand new set were purchased. From the price paid, we can deduce that it was a set of twelve, with a tenor 15 in C. The ringers met twice a week to practise change ringing on them. It would be interesting to discover the whereabouts of these items of Guild property now!

The Bradfield Deanery Branch was founded at this time by Revd. C. H. Travers, the rural dean. He was anxious to start one off and encouraged Revd. J. B. Burne, rector of Wasing, to become the branch secretary. Five towers joined – Bradfield, Burghfield, Englefield, Pangbourne and Theale, and of the forty-three ringers, only six could plain hunt and so were eligible for full membership.

Great efforts were being made in many directions to enlarge the boundaries of the Guild. The Oxford ringers, under Field and Francombe, visited Burford to enrol seventeen new members. Their expenses for the trip came to £2 5s, so the Guild funds were the poorer by £1 8s after this! David Francombe evidently found the pace too much for him, for he wrote to Dolben Paul, asking to be relieved of the secretaryship of the Oxford City Branch. It couldn't have involved him in much work, for the branch had been wound up – at his suggestion – six months earlier!

Towards the end of January seven ringers representing all four Reading towers were joined by Frederick White of Appleton in a peal at Sonning, where he conducted one of his own compositions of Grandsire Triples. Another eighteen months were to elapse before the Reading Branch managed to accomplish a peal on their own, this time at St. Paul's, Wokingham.

In the Cuddesdon deanery Revd. H. J. Ellison was trying to encourage change ringing, but meeting with little success, mainly due to a lack of books. He was unable to buy a copy of Troyte's *Change Ringing* as it was out of print then. He wrote to Dolben Paul, appealing for help and Paul responded by sending his own copy. Their efforts came to nothing apparently, for it was many years before a branch was established in that area.

The problem of teaching change ringing had to be overcome and in the early part of 1882 the Committee made an important decision. Paid instructors were to be appointed, who would travel round the diocese, giving lessons where necessary. Up to half the instructors' expenses would be paid by the Guild, the remainder would be met by the branch or tower needing their services. After some deliberation Joseph Field, of New College, Oxford, was appointed principal instructor, with eight others to assist him in areas he could not conveniently reach. Four men were appointed eight-bell instructors: William Newell of Reading; Frederick White of Appleton; Charles Hounslow of Oxford; and J. R. Haworth of Clerkenwell. Haworth was not a member of the Guild, but he was so highly regarded as a teacher that Dolben Paul invited him to join! The six-bell instructors were J. W. Washbrook, only seventeen years old, of Oxford; W. Bradford of Dunsden, Reading; J. J. Parker of Farnham Royal; and R. Smith of Maidenhead.

William Newell was a little doubtful about being an instructor; initially he declined although he changed his mind later. J. R. Haworth said he would give instruction occasionally and was quickly employed by the Sonning Deanery Branch for one week every three months. He gave a lesson to every tower in the branch and was paid £20 plus £2 expenses. The Guild funds met half of this, the branch chairman paid £5 and the branch contributed the remainder. The value to the branch was considerable, both in expertise and encouragement, and the number of change ringers increased from twenty-four to fifty during the year. At their Annual General Meeting, all the ringing members turned up, except the band from Sandhurst.

The only other branch to take advantage of the scheme at the outset was the Bradfield Deanery; they had two lessons, at a cost to the Guild of a guinea.

The first report was issued about May 1882. Despite some excellent work by Revd. H. C. Sturges who circulated every tower with a request for information about ringing times and the weight of the tenor, it proved to be very inaccurate. Edwin Rogers, of Maidenhead, complained about it and also presented a gloomy picture of ringing in the East Berks and South Bucks branch. The secretary of the Newbury branch was pessimistic too; he saw little likelihood of extending the branch to any other tower in the near future. Better news came from the Woodstock and Steeple Claydon areas; they wanted to start branches but finally settled for just joining the Guild.

The festival took place in July at Oxford and was attended by more than half the ringing members. Perhaps the attraction was the free lunch for those living outside Oxford; they also paid "picnic" fares on the trains on production of their dinner tickets. The events were covered by a number of local papers, including the Reading and Bicester ones, as well as a report in *The Guardian*. Commenting on this *The Bell News* said how gratifying it was to have a church newspaper of such rank and status printing accounts of ringing meetings. One hundred and ninety people sat down to lunch in Christ Church Great Hall, following the Annual General Meeting in the Chapter House. The ringing heard during the day was poor, although it was well-organised, with instructors at all the towers. Most people there had little experience of ringing on bells other than their own.

During the remainder of the year several new methods were added to the peal records. Charles Hounslow called a peal of Kent Treble Bob Major at Kirtlington with the Oxford ringers, and later on one of Grandsire Caters at Christ Church. The Master conducted Stedman Caters at Appleton with the local band, who also rang Union Triples with George Holifield conducting.

These peals were all by some of the more experienced ringers in the Guild. Less ambitous but perhaps more meritorious was Taylor's peal of

Grandsire Triples at Boyne Hill, conducted by William Garraway, which was rung by the local band and was a first for all of them.

At the end of the year the Secretary reported an increase in membership from 313 to 502; there were then 32 towers affiliated. The Sonning branch was the largest, with Bradfield second, followed by the East Berks and South Bucks, Reading and finally Newbury. When he was called to address the Diocesan Conference on the progress of the Guild, Dolben Paul was able to confirm that its objects were being fulfilled.

In a diocese the size of Oxford it is understandable that some ringers would not be prepared to travel long distances to the Annual General Meeting. In 1883 it was decided to hold this meeting at Windsor to encourage the ringers there. Meetings were not held on Saturdays – the inaugural meeting had been on a Monday, the first Annual General Meeting had been on a Wednesday and the second on a Tuesday. Thursday 26th July was selected for the third and a record number attended.

As trains ran late, some of the ringers missed a splendid sermon from Canon W. Wigram, rector of St. Andrew, Hertford, who was a practical ringer and author of *Change Ringing Disentangled.* He had a poor reputation as a striker and the following remark originated about him: "he only made one good blow in a peal, and that was when he missed his sally!" His first peal of Superlative was in his home tower, conducted by Washbrook, with Coleridge and Robinson in the band. In *Among the Bells,* Robinson added a footnote "a very able piece of conducting" while Coleridge described the performance in his peal book as "the worst peal in which I took part."

Despite his deficiencies as a ringer, Wigram was a very able preacher who understood his congregation. An abridged version of his address appeared in *Church Bells,* and could perhaps be delivered at a Festival today to good effect.

Several interesting topics arose at the meeting. The Rules were altered to allow only members of the Church of England to join. It was arranged to issue a certificate to all affiliated towers, and to print a belfry prayer for use before ringing. St. Thomas, Oxford, applied for a grant for restoring their bells, which was refused for the Rules did not allow for such a contingency. A suggestion was made that part of the time at meetings should be devoted to lectures by experienced ringers, some on elementary topics and others on more advanced themes such as "in and out of course." The account does not indicate how much support there was for this idea, and it was never put into practice.

Six towers were open for ringing: the eights at St. John and the Curfew tower, the sixes at Slough, Old Windsor and Wraysbury and the five at Clewer. The principal method was said to be Stedman. At a subsequent meeting in the Newbury branch a complaint was made that did not reach the officers. Apparently some ringers did not manage any ringing on A.G.M. day because of the shortage of towers! In the miscellaneous performances columns of *The Bell News,* 882 and 504 Grandsire Triples were rung at St. John's and 741 Grandsire Triples and 504 Stedman Triples at the Castle. Fifteen ringers participated in these touches, so it isn't surprising that the other 170 present could not catch hold.

Of the nine tower bell peals rung that year, two were by the Appleton band, two by the Oxford ringers, and two by a composite band from the Reading towers, including the first by an all Reading team. The remaining three peals of Grandsire Triples were rung by the Boyne Hill band, with one or two additions. After the peal at Fulham, they all visited the Fisheries Exhibition!

The parochial attitude of some towers was still very strong and their ringers were easily offended over trifling matters, causing many problems and occasionally the withdrawal of a band from the Guild. In 1882 Robinson wrote a tactless letter about the poor rehanging of the bells of St. Lawrence's, Reading to the Vicar; he and his ringers were so upset that most of them left the Guild. In the autumn the ringers at St. Mary's, Reading, instituted a "closed shop," and did not allow any branch practices. This action aggravated the situation for the branch's keen young change ringing members had no eight bell tower to use. The first peal for the branch had to be rung at St. Paul's, Wokingham.

The resentment in Reading simmered on in 1883; no practices were held, no notices distributed nor subscriptions collected. Such a state of affairs clearly could not continue. Early in 1884 Dolben Paul called a meeting for the incumbents of all four churches and most of their ringers. There was a heated discussion with much criticism directed at St. Lawrence's. They were accused of taking advantage of the Guild, for their ringers joined in the branch practices and visited other towers, but would not let the Guild have the use of St. Lawrence's bells.

One of the band agreed, stating that they did not consider change ringing the primary object of church ringers. St. Lawrence's had very strict belfry rules and one was that each member should be a communicant. He felt that the high moral tone of their belfry might be lowered if all and sundry were permitted to ring there. This was a wily argument; the churchmen present could hardly reject such high principles. The vicar of St. Giles remarked drily that his band had properly applied rules too; practices were attended by decent, orderly men.

The meeting adjourned so that St. Lawrence's could discuss the invitation to join the branch. Ten days later, when they resumed, William Newell, the branch secretary, reported that a majority had opposed being affiliated. As a member of St. Lawrence's himself, he was most concerned and thought he should resign as branch secretary. If a member of the clergy were willing to take the post, it would free him to try to dispel the ill-feeling in the town. Fortunately Canon Coleridge was soon to become curate at Caversham and Newell agreed to continue until his arrival. One indignant member claimed that the meeting had not grappled with the chief grievance. Would Guild towers now close their doors to St. Lawrence's ringers? The rural dean smoothed ruffled feathers by admitting the justice of the proposal, but deprecated any course that might savour of retaliation.

An extraordinary remark was made at this Guild meeting by the captain of St. Lawrence's. He announced that though the tower was closed to the Guild, other people might ring there if they obtained the usual consent! The branch's problem reached national fame in May 1884 when two consecutive editorials of *The Bell News* were devoted to them.

Both sides carried on independently, and both prospered! Coleridge became the new branch secretary and some years later Robinson proposed a toast to him at the Oxford University Society dinner, hailing him as "The saviour of the Reading Branch." St. Mary's left the Guild for a couple of years and rejoined in 1888. Caversham went from strength to strength. St. Lawrence's continued, arranging excursions and ringing trips to local towers, some outside the county, and did not become affiliated until 1898.

William Newell, who acted as peace-maker in the district, was an interesting character. Born on 8th November, 1898 at Brightwell, Oxon., the son of the village blacksmith, he learned to ring at South Stoke when he was eleven; he had to walk six miles to and fro for each practice. In 1851 he started work in Reading, where he lodged with his uncle under the shadow of St. Mary's tower. Naturally he joined the band there, but the standard of ringing in Reading was low and he made little progress until 1870 when he met the Appleton and Oxford ringers. He soon made use of his expertise in teaching a band at each of the four Reading towers in turn.

Newell was a brewer and licensed victualler and his house, The Mitre in Broad Street, was a noted resort for ringers. His skill as a teacher led to his appointment as a Guild instructor, a post he held for many years. He was not a prolific peal ringer and most of those he rang were Grandsire Triples or Caters. Of particular note, was the peal he called at St. Lawrence's in 1883, the first peal by a local band for one hundred and fifty years, and a "William" peal of Grandsire in 1885.

In May 1885 he invited all the Reading ringers to his house to dinner; forty-six accepted and enjoyed a first-rate evening. His handbell band, the Royal Berks Handbell Ringers, provided the entertainment on his set of fifty bells.

The Guild was active in the sphere of tower inspections. Robinson's forthright comments on the rehanging of St. Lawrence's caused ill-feeling; normally such inspections did nothing but good. The vicar of Bray asked for an experienced ringer to look at his bells which had just been rehung by Warners. Dolben Paul asked Haworth to undertake this job and he reported meeting the bell hangers, trying the bells and advising the locals not to settle the account until the bells were made pealable! The Bray ringers were so pleased with this help that they promptly joined the Guild.

David Francombe still regarded himself as the secretary of the non-existent Oxford City branch; he requested the Guild to buy a set of muffles for the use of ringers in his area. Dolben Paul, usually good-natured in his dealings with members, would only pay for them if Francombe agreed to collect the subscriptions again and guarantee that the muffles would be used by Guild members only. Needless to say, this item never appeared in the Guild accounts!

The 1884 Annual General Meeting was going to be held at Newbury. Encouragement was needed in the branch, for although it had been founded two years earlier, only members from Newbury tower had come to any of the meetings. Thatcham joined in '84 and were progressing favourably with their change ringing. They had borrowed the second set of handbells to practise on – these were the ones the Newbury band had rejected as not being good enough! The branch declined the request for the meeting to be held at Newbury because their bells were "unfit for ringing!" The second choice, Abingdon, was also turned down, so Great Marlow was selected.

Tuesday, 22nd July was a gloriously sunny day and many of the ringers found it hard to decide whether to ring or to stroll along the bank of the Thames, listening to the bells. Some even took a punt out on the river! The service and meeting followed the now well-established pattern; dinner was served in the grounds of the Greyhound Hotel. Ringing took place at the surrounding towers, and the delights of the water attracted some people away from the ropes.

Dolben Paul was most insistent that members should be on their best behaviour for Guild functions. He heard that one wagon-load of ringers stopped for a boisterous drinking session at Maidenhead on their way home; he asked their incumbent to deal with them! This worthy cleric duly confirmed that "they had been spoken to." Their excuse was that they had been led astray by one of the older ringers who'd accompanied them and he wasn't a member of the Guild!

Occasionally Dolben Paul met with disappointment. Having successfully launched a small branch and then a large Guild, he aimed even higher – at a national association. He tried to persuade Church Congress to discuss ringing associations at its meeting in Reading in 1883. When his request was refused, he arranged a ringers' conference for the same week with the help of Canon W. Wigram, Jasper Snowdon and J. E. Troyte. A large number of ringers came, with some of the clergy, and a committee was formed to draft a scheme for a national association. Dolben Paul was its secretary and pursued the project with his usual vigour, circulating all the societies and associations in the country for their comments. Universal approval was not forthcoming; the College Youths said they did not want one, and furthermore, wouldn't have one! Eventually Dolben Paul appealed for a response from those in favour through the columns of *The Bell News*. He was bitterly disappointed to receive only fifteen replies, and concluded that the time was not yet ripe for such an enterprise. By the time the Central Council was formed, he was too ill to know about it.

The number of peals steadily increased and the majority were rung by the old hands, although a few new names crept in. The Oxford ringers went to Long Crendon to help two of the local band through a peal of Grandsire Triples. Joseph Field carried out his job as chief instructor admirably; seven of the band he taught at Burford rang their first peal together with him conducting. These ringers called themselves the Burford Branch and reported their activities to *The Bell News* under that name, although they were never recognised as such by the Guild.

The Master called the first peal of Double Norwich Court Bob Major for the Guild with ringers from Oxford and Appleton. He also called a peal of Stedman Caters at St. Lawrence, Reading – rather a surprise in view of all the controversy! The remaining peals in 1884 were all Grandsire or Stedman Triples by the Maidenhead, Reading, Oxford or Appleton bands.

There was more variety in the peals in '85 and Washbrook's talents as a first-class conductor were developing swiftly. He called fourteen peals for the Guild, twice his grand total up to that time. Amongst these were several of his own compositions: a variation of Thurstan's peal of Stedman, a five part peal of Grandsire Triples and one of Bob Major. The latter was the first peal in the method for the Guild and the first for all the band. Robinson called the first peal of Superlative for the Guild with a band from Appleton and Oxford; it was the fifteenth peal rung in the method. Earlier in the year he had rung, in the ninth peal of Superlative with the Burton-on-Trent ringers.

The fashion of inviting bands to open bells after rehanging was still very popular and Robinson was asked to take a Guild band to Taunton after Taylors had augmented the bells to a ring of ten. Before the service they raised the bells in peal and rang nine courses of Stedman Caters in "splendid style." After a celebratory lunch, they returned to the tower and rang 5,079 Stedman Caters, conducted by Robinson. The peal was published in *The Bell News* but never appeared in the Guild records. Seven years later Robinson withdrew his peal, as it was false. He claimed that one of the band had sent it up without his permission. He did apologise for his delay in retracting it!

Washbrook was a six-bell instructor and one of the bands that he taught was at Drayton St. Leonard, Oxon. All the ringers worked on the estate of H. D. Betteridge Esq., and during 1885 they rang two peals at Drayton, Berks. The first was Holt's Original and was the first peal for all the band apart from their instructor. Two months later they returned, each to ring the same bell, for their first of Stedman Triples – a remarkable effort!

William Newell helped start the band at East Hagbourne. The bells were rehung by Whites of Appleton in 1883 but "the ups and downs and rounds and rounds" persisted until the next year when they acquired a set of handbells and had instruction from Newell. Six months later they achieved their first 120 of Grandsire Doubles with 6, 7, 8 behind. Soon Washbrook called their first peal of Grandsire Triples and within a couple of months they were ringing peals on their own.

The Festival and Annual General Meeting for 1885 was held at Bicester on Tuesday 9th June. This area was chosen because Revd. W. Draper, vicar of Middleton Stoney, was trying to organise a branch in this otherwise dead part of the diocese. Nearly 200 people attended and the event was covered by reporters from the three Oxford papers, the two Bicester papers and *The Banbury Guardian*. The sermon was preached by Revd. C. D. P. Davies, who was then at Pembroke College, Oxford. Dolben Paul reported at the meeting that the Guild was now the largest in the country with over 800 members, for 150 new members had joined during the year. The now familiar process of electing non-resident life members before a peal was first suggested; it met with some opposition but was accepted finally. The Earl of Jersey presented a peal book: speeches were made and an excellent dinner enjoyed.

Five towers were open for ringing: Middleton Stoney, Marsh Gibbon, Launton, Ambrosden and Bicester. Twenty ringers went by brake to Middleton Stoney for a brief ring. They didn't excel themselves in the tower so they adjourned to Lord Jersey's gardens and were entertained to tea! The Stoney Stratford band, who had just become members, decided to go to Ambrosden and the article in *The Bicester Herald* stated that there "they accomplished nothing of note." They vindicated their honour, however, by ringing 120 Grandsire Doubles at Bicester before they caught the train home.

Among the nineteen peals rung in 1885 was one in seven Minor methods by the Caversham band; this was the first six bell peal by all the band and for the Guild, and was conducted by Revd. G. F. Coleridge. With Thomas Newman he steered this band to great heights. In the following years 33 peals were rung, including several deserving special attention. Early in the year J. Martin Routh called the first peal on the augmented bells at Tilehurst; he proved himself a great asset to the Bradfield Branch. The band from St. Giles, Reading had an excursion to Englefield where they rang a peal in seven Minor methods.

This effort may have been inspired by the example of the Drayton St. Leonard ringers. Some months earlier, under Washbrook's conductorship, they had rung 7,200 changes in seven methods in four hours, the longest peal for the Guild. Later they visited Drayton, Berks., where Robinson and Washbrook joined them to ring two peals of Double Norwich within the space of five days – tremendous progress for a small village band. At Burford the locals rang their first peal without Joseph Field, who had moved to Devon and was acting as instructor to the Guild of Devonshire Ringers.

Abingdon was a centre of Guild activity just then. The bells of St. Helen's were augmented to ten and were opened by a Guild band on 1st May. A peal of Stedman Caters was attempted, but after eleven courses had been rung in just under an hour, it was clear that the ringers of the back two bells would be unable to finish the peal. Ringing was abandoned and the bell hangers recalled. Four weeks later the problems were rectified and a successful peal was brought round.

Abingdon was the venue for the Festival and Annual General Meeting, attended by more than three hundred people. Lunch was served in a marquee in the Abbey grounds. One interesting item of business at the meeting was a grant of £5 to Holywell, Oxford for their augmentation to eight. The money was paid, but the work was never carried out.

The work of the instructors continued to provide practical help. Frederick White had retired and his place was taken by George Holifield, also of Appleton. W. Bradford had been replaced by William Garraway from Boyne Hill and G. Warner of Long Crendon had been pressed into service. The Guild paid the instructors' fees for eight towers; £17 was spent from central funds and an equivalent sum was contributed by the branches and towers concerned.

Administratively, the Guild now had a "University" branch, which seems to have been a private arrangement with Dolben Paul for collecting subscriptions. For the whole year these amounted to 6s od. The branch had a secretary, but no representative on the Guild Committee, and the name faded away in the following year.

Forty-eight peals were rung in 1887, an increase of fifteen on the previous year. The quality of the methods rung was steadily improving; one of Cambridge, three of Superlative, six of Double Norwich and seventeen of Stedman. Although two dozen or so new names appeared in the peal columns, most of the peals were rung by the well-established peal bands. The Cambridge Major was the first for the Guild and was rung by a band from Appleton strengthened by Hounslow and Washbrook, and conducted by Robinson. It is interesting that he considered himself an Appleton ringer, despite having a band of probationers at Drayton!

The benefits of instruction could be seen to have an effect. Washbrook called a peal at Dorchester with five local men ringing their first peal; a fortnight later he returned there to call another peal for the rest of the band. Beenham had had some instruction, probably from William Newell, and so were able to accomplish a peal of Bob Minor in the autumn. This was recorded as "the first on the bells, and by all the band, who are all self-taught and have only been change ringing twelve months."

Washbrook was the leading conductor and called thirty-six peals. One of his feats was to call a peal of Stedman Triples at Henley from the tenor, the first time this had been done. He was particularly proud of another peal of Stedman, rung at St. Andrew's, Cambridge. Robinson had been invited to take a band to Mildenhall, Suffolk to open the bells with a peal, which was lost in the last six changes – a trip stopped the bells running round. On the way home they went for the peal at St. Andrew's; Robinson recorded how delighted they were that an Oxford band rang the first peal of Stedman at Cambridge, Stedman's birthplace.

Two other peals are worth mentioning. One was 6,048 Superlative at Drayton, the longest peal in the method for the Guild and a first in the method for five of the band. The second was at Newbury where Washbrook conducted the usual Stedman Triples with a band mostly from Appleton. It was the first peal on the bells and Robinson noted that the natives thought three hours' ringing would prove fatal to the ringers, and were prepared to wager that none of them would come out of the tower alive. After the peal an old woman patted him on the back and said "Well, you be alive then! Now, never do the like of that, never no more!"

The stark details of a peal don't convey much of the background. On. 22nd April, 1887, Washbrook called Holt's Original at Hagbourne; that is all the Report records. It doesn't indicate that this formed part of an attempt for three peals in a day. Uncommon now, it was extremely rare then, and this is one of the first known instances.

The band began at six in the morning and scored the first peal at Hagbourne. Then they walked to Dorchester where a peal of Stedman was lost after two hours fifteen minutes' ringing. After a short rest they re-crossed the Thames and walked to Drayton where they were unlucky again. A rope broke a minute from the end.

With the Guild's influence many bands were progressing. Burford's active band were on to Bob Major and the Caversham band were ringing 720s in many methods. In September they had a very successful non-ringing outing to London, where they saw Buffalo Bill's Wild West Show, Warner's Foundry and then enjoyed a trip on a steamer! In the preceding twelve months they had rung a total of 62,667 changes in nine methods. With such an achievement it is no wonder they earned the title of the premier six-bell band in the Guild.

The Annual General Meeting and Festival were at High Wycombe; one vital decision taken was that the maximum price for beer in the beer tent would be threepence a pint!

The year closed with the membership at 945, of whom nearly 200 were honorary members. The tower with the largest number of ringers was Great Marlow, who listed the names of thirty-nine ringing members including only nine probationers. It would be hard to find a tower today with such an extensive band.

Chapter Six

WASHBROOK'S YEAR

"Mr Washbrook gave his whole time to bell ringing."
"Among the Bells"

In his ringing diary Revd. F. E. Robinson described 1888 as one of the busiest years of his ringing career, as Washbrook devoted his whole time to ringing. Of all the great exponents of the Exercise, Washbrook is the man whose name will remain evergreen. He was only twenty-three in that year, but he had already demonstrated his skill, and had no equal among his contemporaries. It is probably true to say that no one has equalled his all-round genius as a ringer, composer and conductor.

James William Washbrook was born at Kidlington on 27th July 1864, and taught himself to ring at St Thomas', Oxford while he was a boy. He made rapid progress and his first peal was the first for the Guild. Within a short time his extraordinary talent became apparent and he was appointed one of the Guild's instructors while still in his 'teens. This may not seem unusual now, but in the latter part of the nineteenth century anyone under twenty-one was still a boy, and would be held in little regard by older men. He made an ideal instructor; besides his undoubted ability, he was affable, modest and retiring and got on well with people. In the belfry he was calm, clear-headed, confident and determined.

He first came to the fore as a conductor. The stories told of his skill are legion, and no doubt time has embellished them. In one recorded exploit, he shepherded three men through 3,900 Stedman Triples in an attempt for a peal, although none of them had struck a blow in the method before. On another occasion his band met one short for a peal of Surprise Major; a local replacement was found for the treble, and the treble ringer, who could only ring Kent "inside," was talked through a peal of Superlative!

Washbrook was not large in stature yet he had great physical strength. His hands were huge — he could span an octave and a half on the piano with ease — and with his dexterity, he made heavy bell ringing look simple. Examples of this arise later in his career; he was often called in to perform feats that were considered impossible. Equally at home on a light bell, his versatility made him very much in demand for all the peal tours just coming into fashion.

He excelled in the art of composition. An eminent present-day composer has suggested that his ringing abilities "were matched by his genius as a composer." His variation of Middleton's peal provided a welcome alternative to Johnson's, as did the three part peal of Cambridge with the tenors split. He composed a number of peals of Stedman Triples, replacing the extras and omits found in all the contemporary twin bob peals with Singles. In the presence of Charlie Hounslow he joked that he had just called Thurstan's peal without extras or omits, and was delighted by the other's concern for its truth.

On 28th January the first peal of more than ten thousand changes was rung for the Guild; this performance was 10,080 Double Norwich Court Bob Major in five hours fifty-eight minutes at Appleton. The band stood: R. White Treble, E Holifield 2, C. Hounslow 3, W. Bennett 4, J. Avery 5, Revd. F. E. Robinson 6, G. Holifield 7, and J. W. Washbrook tenor, composed and conducted by J. W. Washbrook.

Five weeks later, for Appleton's "4th March" celebrations, 12,041 Stedman Caters were rung in seven hours twenty-six minutes with the following band:

APPLETON, Berks.

On 5th March 1888 in 7 hours 26 minutes

12,041 STEDMAN CATERS

F. White .... Treble	G. Holifield 6
G. H. Phillott 2	Revd. F. E. Robinson 7
E. Holifield 3	J. Avery 8
W. Bennett 4	J. W. Washbrook 9
H. Baker 5	F. S. White .... Tenor

Composed and conducted by J. W. Washbrook

This was then the longest peal rung in the method, for it surpassed the "five ones" peal, 11,111 changes rung at Fulham by the College Youths in 1883.

On Easter Monday a band was despatched to Wells to open the bells at St. Cuthbert's, and the first peal to be rung in the city of Wells was credited to the Guild. They attempted to ring at the Cathedral — it normally took eleven men to ring them to rounds — and although they accomplished a good 504 Grandsire Triples, it took three local men to ring the tenor. Washbrook tried to ring it on his own, but had to confess himself beaten when he couldn't set it! Another peal was rung the following day at Glastonbury. Charlie Houslow, who was on the expedition, refused to enter Glastonbury tower because he distrusted the overhanging pinnacles!

The next weekend another record length was successfully attempted — 13,247 Grandsire Caters in eight hours five minutes. The band was the same as for the Stedman Caters, apart from Hounslow replacing Phillott. With this peal the Guild achieved the record length on ten bells. *The Bell News* report described the striking as "simply perfection from beginning to end, not a word other than 'Bob' being spoken for hours . . ." Both these peals were in the tittums throughout, the turning course being the homing course.

Another record fell two days later when a peal of Stedman Triples was brought round in two hours twenty-seven minutes at Drayton and was claimed as the fastest peal on tower bells. Some comments were provoked in the correspondence columns of *The Bell News,* where insinuations of "cooking" the peal were made against the conductor. Robinson countered by attesting the truth and good striking of the peal and offered to ring it again for the critics, which silenced them effectively.

That summer the weather was hot and not really conducive to peal ringing. Washbrook decided, however, to try for three peals in a day again; wisely he elected to ring them all in one tower. The band met at Drayton at six o'clock, hoping to ring the first in the cool of the morning. Cambridge Major was lost after two and a half hours' ringing when one of the ropes slipped wheel. After breakfast at the vicarage, the band returned to the tower and successfully accomplished peals of Cambridge, Superlative and Double Norwich. Robinson noted "a busy day during which we spent ten and a quarter hours ringing nearly 20,000 changes."

The Cheltenham band surpassed the Stedman Caters record after only eleven weeks with a peal of 13,054 changes. Washbrook was determined to retrieve the record and assembled his band at Appleton on 31st December at nine in the morning. They were horrified to find that Jesse Avery, one of the locals, hadn't appeared! A messenger rushed off to the next village, where he was discovered peacefully threshing corn in the barn. He had completely forgotten about the peal but walked to Appleton after ensuring a substitute continued his work.

The peal went into changes at ten-thirty, and the ringing was excellent until about four o'clock when one of the band went in quick instead of slow. The rhythm was upset temporarily but the even striking was resumed after a few sixes until another trip occurred at six o'clock. Once again the band rallied and the final hour and a half's ringing was first-class.

APPLETON, Berks.
On 31st December 1888, in 9 hours 16 minutes.
15,041 STEDMAN CATERS

F. White	Treble	Revd. F. E. Robinson	6
C. Hounslow	2	J. Avery	7
H. Baker	3	J. W. Washbrook	8
W. Bennett	4	Revd. G. F. Coleridge	9
G. Holifield	5	F. S. White	Tenor

Composed and conducted by J. W. Washbrook.

This peal contained the greatest number of changes ever rung on ten bells and was destined to remain the record for the next thirty years. William Pye's band beat it when he called 18,027 Stedman Caters from the thirty hundredweight tenor of Loughborough Parish Church — a truly remarkable feat by another great ringer.

These long lengths tend to overshadow the other peals rung that year. The local band at Slough rang a peal of Plain Bob Triples, the first for the Guild. The Minor band at Beenham extended their repertoire to seven different methods. Washbrook rang peals with local bands at Abingdon, Boyne Hill and East Hagbourne and was in fifty-three of sixty-four peals rung for the Guild that year. His personal total was 121, by far the highest ever scored then in a twelve month; his closest rival was probably Robinson with sixty-nine.

The Guild had helped Washbrook to reach this point. In 1887 he had been appointed instructor to the Hereford Diocesan Guild and the Committee were determined to retain his services in the subsequent year. Accordingly they appointed him principal instructor, or, as one report put it, permanent instructor; he was engaged for six months at thirty shillings a week. With such an expense the number of instructors had to be reduced and Messrs. Newell, Haworth and Smith were kept on. Their duties were restricted to acting as substitutes for Washbrook. J. J. Parker was one of the instructors who was dropped; it may have been a fit of pique over this which made Farnham Royal withdraw from the Guild.

Washbrook was also a skilled handbell ringer. In the early days of the Guild he was trying to teach a band in Oxford to ring Grandsire Triples; it was November 1882 before the first quarter was scored. Over the next six months regular peal attempts were made none of which exceeded two thousand changes. Finally on 18th June 1883 Washbrook called Holt's Ten-Part. The other ringers were the two Hounslow brothers and W. C. Baston. In October they went on to ring Holt's Original.

In the Newbury area handbell ringing was encouraged by Revd. J. M. Bacon, who held a competition at his house at Cold Ash in 1885 for tune and change ringing. William Newell was the judge; Lambourn won the call change competition and Abingdon the change ringing.

The next handbell peal of note was rung at Burford. A fund had been started for recasting the fifth bell and a garden party was arranged. As an added attraction Washbrook was invited to ring a handbell peal in a little summerhouse in the grounds, where all the visitors could stroll by and see the ringing. With such distractions, it is surprising that 5,021 Grandsire Caters was successfully brought round. The band was the same as for the first peal in hand, with the addition of Joseph Field.

The first peal of Bob Major was achieved by the Reading ringers in February 1886; it was conducted by G. Gibbard and was rung single-handed. Amongst the band were A. E. Reeves and R. T. Hibbert, two future secretaries of the Guild. Simultaneously Washbrook's band was working up to a peal of Stedman Triples. They were successful after four tries, two of them reaching nearly four and a half thousand changes before coming to grief. The final attempt was rung in Magdalen tower and was the first handbell peal of Stedman to be accomplished outside London.

Washbrook considered tapping a handbell peal, having heard no doubt of the marvellous ability of Elijah Roberts who died in 1865. The latter had tapped many peals of Maximus and Cinques and the peals were conducted and witnessed by many well-known ringers of that era. His finest peal was 19,440 Kent Treble Bob Maximus, which he completed in thirteen hours forty-three minutes in 1832. Washbrook tapped several 720s in various Minor methods, and also courses of Cinques and Maximus. He also used to play these on the piano as his party piece! For some reason he never tried to tap a peal.

The only handbell peal in 1888 was at Great Marlow where he had been instructing. He met the Truss family who had been ringing handbells for some time. J. C. Truss Jnr., who became one of the best handbell ringers produced by the branch, was then nearly fourteen years old and rang 7-8 to Holt's Original. The peal was umpired by another member of the family, who marked off each lead-end as it came up.

Up to the year 1900 Washbrook conducted all the double-handed handbell peals for the Guild. It would be many years before another conductor would make such a contribution in this field.

Chapter Seven

THE END OF THE DECADE

As the Guild approached the end of its first ten years of existence it was still expanding and consolidating its position. More peals were being rung, mainly through the diligence of its principal instructor. The band he taught at Hughenden rang peals of Grandsire, Stedman Triples, and Bob Major, all with him conducting. A little later they were ringing local peals with John Evans, one of the band, as conductor. He had a fairly meteoric rise to eminence; he rang his first peal in February 1889, conducted his first later that year and became a Guild Instructor in 1891. He also called the first peal of Double Norwich Court Bob Major to be rung in Buckinghamshire, again with the Hughenden band.

Washbrook was busy in other towers. At Newbury he called a peal of Grandsire Triples for the locals and another at Great Marlow for their band. He conducted the first peal of Stedman Triples for the Boyne Hill band — on this occasion Robinson helped out! At Ducklington the local band all rang Grandsire Doubles for their first peal. It was also the first peal in the tower and a first in the method for the Guild.

J. J. Parker took some of his band from Farnham Royal on a visit to Hillingdon, just a few miles away. Here they rang one of his compositions of Oxford Bob Triples, another "first" for the Guild and all the band. Another interesting peal was one of Duffield Major; Sir Arthur Heywood, the composer, had averred it was impossible to ring a peal in the method without prior practice. Washbrook thought differently, and, with his usual peal band, accomplished it with ease at the first attempt.

In 1888 the Guild held its Annual General Meeting at Witney and in the following year they were at Newbury. Dolben Paul had pleasure in announcing that the membership total now exceeded a thousand, the first time an association had reached such a high number. He clashed with Robinson over a motion about probationary members. The latter wanted to introduce a rule limiting to two years the period a ringer could be a probationer, suggesting that permanent probationers should be promoted to honorary membership, paying five shillings a year for the privilege rather than a shilling. "If those members will not help the Guild with their brains, it is only fair that they should do so with their money." The motion was defeated after strong representations had been made against it by Dolben Paul.

The Bell News devoted an editorial to this topic, commenting on the far-sightedness of the secretary as opposed to the narrow view taken by the Master; a proposition to "fine" a member because he was unable to make himself efficient was unwise. The article indicated that Robinson would be far better occupied in teaching a band in his own parish rather than devoting so much of his time to peal ringing. "To utilise his knowledge energetically for the benefit of others not so skilled as himself would, we venture to say, be of more value to the Exercise generally, and the Oxford Guild in particular, than if he were to ring four peals a day for the rest of his life."

This was, perhaps, a little unfair on Robinson, who had little aptitude for teaching. He could be rude, stern and overbearing, qualities which do not evince a good response from learners. He may also have found it difficult to mix with people he considered socially inferior. He enjoyed peal ringing and was keen to increase his total, especially as he grew older. Even so he had set standards; he would not ring a peal in Lent, and although in some of his later peals the striking was sometimes suspect, he was a stickler for the truth of the performance.

One example of his rudeness is often quoted concerning his birthday peals. Each year he would attempt a peal of Stedman Triples at Drayton on his birthday, and afterwards he would entertain the band to supper at the vicarage. This had been the custom for many years and the ringers looked forward to the spread. One day the peal attempts were unsuccessful and as it was too late for them to try again, they donned their coats and trooped round to the house, to be greeted by Robinson on the threshold with "Well, gentlemen, no peal — no supper!" With that he shut the door on them.

In one sphere his qualities were put to good use, for on average he visited about twelve towers a year, inspecting the bells and gear. He then made recommendations to the vicar about what action should be taken to put the bells in working order. In October 1890 he attended the reopening of the recast six at Padworth, Berks. He did not care for the tone of the tenor, so at his "request" Mears and Stainbank replaced the bell, presumably at no small cost to themselves!

The number of peals rung in the first year of the nineties dropped considerably, possibly through the indisposition of Washbrook. In the autumn he had a serious illness; when he appeared to be on the road to recovery he suffered a relapse and spent over a month in the Oxford Infirmary. Collections were made at branch meetings and sent to him in appreciation of his services to the Guild. Earlier in the year he was able to fulfil his job as principal instructor, helping the band at Woodstock to ring their first peal of Grandsire Triples. More of the huge band at Great Marlow were assisted through a peal.

The eminent Birmingham ringer, Henry Johnson died in January and three peals were rung in his memory — at Christ Church, Drayton, and Appleton. It is worthwhile mentioning a rule that existed for Washbrook's and Robinson's peal band. If you went wrong in the Slow work in Stedman you were fined two shillings and sixpence. Considering that the average farm labourer's wage was only ten shillings a week, this fine must have been a powerful inducement to remain awake!

Several other peals indicate the advances made in change ringing in the diocese. At Ducklington the local band had progressed to ringing peals of Grandsire Doubles with "extremes" as well as Bobs and Singles. At Pangbourne the locals, with help from Whitchurch across the river, accomplished 5,040 Grandsire Doubles, the first by nearly all the band. The Caversham band rang a peal of Minor in fourteen different methods, following it up with the first in seven Treble Bob methods for the Guild.

Other bands were not so fortunate; the Appleton band broke up as some of its members retired from active ringing. Robinson commented upon this in the Report and at the next Annual General Meeting lamenting "the end of all change ringing there." There were several losses by death; one of these was Edwin Rogers, who was born at Hughenden in 1834, where he learned to handle a bell. Later he moved to Boyne Hill and, before taking up change ringing, rang a peal of "call changes" for three hours at Cookham. Although he rang several peals of Grandsire Triples, he spent most of his time teaching. He never tired of going over the same ground again and again; his patience was inexhaustible. One of his favourite homilies was that all ringers should be taught with the same amount of forbearance. He was treasurer of the East Berks and South Bucks branch at the time of his death, and, indeed, had been one of those responsible for establishing it in 1879. He died in April 1890 from cancer of the back.

Another loss to the Guild was its former principal instructor, Joseph Field, a leading Oxford ringer and a competent conductor and excellent striker. He had rung over a hundred peals, including several of Surprise, and some double handed handbell peals. He called the first local peals of Stedman Triples and Caters to be scored in Oxford. Genial and hospitable, he was well-liked by his fellow ringers, qualities which endeared him to the many bands he taught in the Guild, as well as in Devon. He was a store-keeper at New College, and was taken ill while out shopping for the College. He never regained consciousness and died almost at once; he was only forty-seven.

An even more serious loss was that of Dolben Paul; the Minute Book records that he was unable to be present at the Annual General Meeting at Buckingham through illness in his family. Soon it became clear that it was he who was ill. He was re-elected secretary and treasurer at the business meeting, but never carried out any further duties. Revd. R. H. Hart-Davis did the work until the following October, when he was officially appointed acting secretary. He wrote to Mrs Paul, expressing the members' gratitude for all her husband's work, and sympathising over his illness. There was Victorian reticence about the nature of this illness; today it would be described as a complete mental breakdown.

At the next Annual General Meeting Robinson paid tribute in a roundabout way, saying the Guild had lost "the services of Mr Paul under whose labours they had begun under very lamentable circumstances. Leaving the office as he did, the Guild and his successor were placed in a peculiar difficulty because he was not there to give any explanation." Revd. A. H. Drummond was more sympathetic: "... a loss from amongst them of one who was a most able servant of the Guild, meaning their excellent friend Mr Dolben Paul, for whom he was perfectly sure all the members of the Guild must be feeling deeply."

After his death in June 1892, the Master's Report carried the following eulogy:

"During the year there has passed to his rest one who has rendered invaluable service to the Guild. The foundation of the Guild was in great measure due to Dolben Paul, and for nine years he actively carried on the duties of secretary. His health, long precarious, failed him in the autumn of 1890, and in June last he died. His memory will be long held in affectionate remembrance by the Bell Ringers of the Oxford Diocesan Guild."

The chart shows how the membership gradually increased with the passing of the decade. The total of honorary and life members hovered around one hundred and eighty-five, while that of the ringing members slowly crept upwards. The Guild's objectives were being achieved.

The first of these stated that ringers should be recognised as church workers. Dolben Paul had worked hard on this, encouraging influential people to join as honorary and life members, so that the standing of the Guild and so its membership would prosper. After attending the enthronement of the Archbishop of Canterbury in 1883, he obtained the prelate's consent to becoming the Guild's Patron. Successive Archbishops remained Patrons for the next fifty years.

The second aim was the promotion of belfry reform, another sphere in which Dolben Paul had exerted a great deal of effort, exhorting clergy throughout the diocese to take an interest in their towers. As the Guild expanded, its influence grew, and the old style of ringer was squeezed out. Although belfry reform was not complete at the end of the decade, a fine start had been made.

The last objective was the promotion of change ringing. The policy of providing paid instructors had proved successful and the ability of Guild members had steadily increased. In 1881 there were four probationers to

Fig. 2   Revd. F. E. Robinson
Master 1881-1910

Fig. 3   Revd. C. W. O. Jenkyn
Deputy Master 1905-1910
Master 1910-1933

Fig. 4 Charles Houslow
Conductor of the first peal rung
for the guild.

Fig. 5 James W. Washbrook
Composer, conductor, brilliant
heavy bellringer. His genius and
ability as an instructor
established the guild as the
leading territorial association of
the time.

Fig. 6 St. Laurence, Appleton, Berks.
Many long lengths have been rung on these bells.

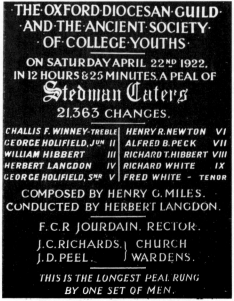

·THE·OXFORD·DIOCESAN·GUILD·
·AND·THE·ANCIENT·SOCIETY·
·OF·COLLEGE·YOUTHS·

ON SATURDAY APRIL 22ND 1922,
IN 12 HOURS & 25 MINUTES, A PEAL OF

Stedman Caters

21,363 CHANGES.

CHALLIS F. WINNEY-TREBLE		HENRY R. NEWTON	VI
GEORGE HOLIFIELD, JUN II		ALFRED B. PECK	VII
WILLIAM HIBBERT	III	RICHARD T. HIBBERT	VIII
HERBERT LANGDON	IV	RICHARD WHITE	IX
GEORGE HOLIFIELD, SNR	V	FRED WHITE -	TENOR

COMPOSED BY HENRY G. MILES.
CONDUCTED BY HERBERT LANGDON.

F.C.R JOURDAIN. RECTOR.

J.C. RICHARDS. | CHURCH
J.D. PEEL. | WARDENS.

THIS IS THE LONGEST PEAL RUNG
BY ONE SET OF MEN.

Fig. 7 Peal board at Appleton.

Fig. 8 The London Surprise Major record band.
From left to right: F. Exon, C. Hounslow, C. H. Fowler, C. H. Exon, J. W.
Washbrook, E. Hims, Revd. F. E. Robinson, T. Payne.

Fig. 9   St. Peter, Drayton, Berks.

Fig. 10   The Olney ringers, circa. 1900.
Standing from left to right: W. Robinson, W. Wright, W. Jones, F. Boswell,
C. Roberts, — ?, J. Perkins. Seated: S. Smith and R. Perkins.

Fig. 11 The Bradfield ringers, 1905.
Standing: C. Giles, A. Lampard, A. W. Pike, A. Standidge, G. Abery.
Seated: J. Abery, Mary Chillingworth, Kate Smith, Caroline Chillingworth,
H. Tucker.

Fig. 12   Alfred E. Reeves.
General Secretary 1911-1917

Fig. 13   Richard T. Hibbert
General Secretary 1917-1945

Fig. 14   Canon G. F. Coleridge
Master 1933-1946

Fig. 15   Canon C. E. Wigg
Deputy Master 1933-1946
Master 1946-1973

Fig. 16   Robinson's 1,000th peal band.

Fig. 17 Challis F. Winney.
One of the guild's first
instructors and a notable College
Youth.

Fig. 18 William Newell.
The "Father" of ringing in
Reading.

Fig. 19   Alice White.
The first woman to ring a peal for
the guild.

Fig. 20   The first ladies peal of
Surprise Major, rung for the
Ladies Guild. Three members of
the Guild took part: Mrs. A. D.
Barker (centre back row), Miss
Stella Davis (extreme left) and
Mrs A. Diserens (right seated).

Fig. 21 SS Peter and Paul, Buckingham.

Fig. 22 St. Mary, Aylesbury.
The first peal in the county by a
local band was rung here in 1804.

Fig. 23 The members at the 1909 Annual General Meeting at Chipping Norton.

Revd. F. E. Robinson may be seen in the centre front, with Revd. C. W. O. Jenkyn beside him. Canon G. F. Coleridge is further to his right, with the Assistant General Secretary, A. E. Reeves, in front of him.

Fig. 24 All Saints, East Garston.
The birth and burial place of Rev. C. W. O. Jenkyn. It was here he learnt to ring.

Fig. 25 SS Peter and Paul, Dorchester.
The first peal in 25 Spliced Surprise Major methods was rung here in 1951.

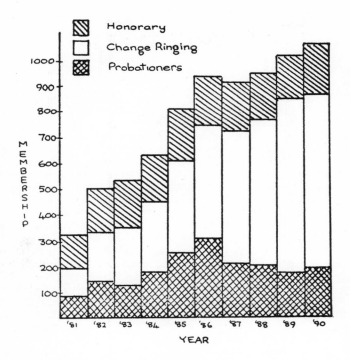

every five change ringers. Five years later it had dropped to three to every four, and by 1890 there were only two rounds ringers to every seven change ringers. The £254 spent on instruction had been a good investment. With a weekly wage of fifteen shillings this works out to 335 weeks of instruction or six and a half years! The Guild would be hard pressed to find £35,000 today for an equivalent amount of time!

Up to the last year of the decade the Sonning Deanery maintained its position as the branch with the largest number of members. Finally the East Berks and South Bucks branch supplanted them; their early start had given them some prominence, although their membership remained small until 1886, when they replaced the Bradfield Deanery as the second largest branch. The troubles in the Reading branch kept their numbers down while the Newbury branch struggled on with about three dozen members. The rest of the nineteenth century would see some important changes.

Chapter Eight

THE END OF AN ERA

In the early days of the Guild's history the clergy had played an important part. Many of them had taken up ringing; the only area not having a clerical secretary was the Newbury branch, and of all five, this was the weakest. Some curates were undoubtedly pushed into ringing. Revd. R. P. Newhouse was at Boyne Hill and his vicar nominated him as secretary of the East Berks and South Bucks branch. He became a very efficient ringer, scoring several peals of Grandsire Triples. His successor, both as curate and secretary, was Revd. H. C. Bell who also rang peals in several Triples methods. Revd. J. H. Hindson, vicar of Wraysbury, was an accomplished ringer, taking part in a number of peals of Stedman Triples. In 1890 he received an invitation to respond to one of the toasts at the College Youths' dinner.

Other men thought it part of their duty to join the men in the belfry. Revd. A. E. Molineux joked that he had been practially forced into the ringing chamber and taught to handle a bell when he first came to Caversham as vicar. He added that it was only the arrival of Revd. G. F. Coleridge as his curate that "prevented" him from becoming a skilful ringer! Another reluctant entrant to the belfry was Revd. T. E. E. Chataway at Woodstock, who was taught by Washbrook and took part in some peals with the local band.

In a previous chapter we have seen how Washbrook was appointed principal instructor, with Newell, Haworth and Smith as his deputies. His illness in 1891 or some other internal cause precipitated a change in the rules later in the year. Bowers, Evans, Lawrence, Parker, Short, Wilkins, and Yates were added to the list of those qualified to act as instructors, all of them on an equal footing. From then to the end of the century the amount spent on instruction gradually decreased, from £41 in 1891 to £8 in 1900. In the ten year period £170 was spent, considerably less than the sum invested before. Times, and men, were changing.

As the Guild gained in stature it received invitations to open rings of bells in towers outside the diocese. Usually these were addressed to Robinson, and sometimes his peal ringing ambitions exceeded his prudence. Such an instance was the re-opening of the bells at Wells Cathedral.

An iron frame and new fittings had been supplied by Blackbourn and Greenleaf of Salisbury. In addition Mears and Stainbank had cast two new bells, making a fine ring of ten. The Report records that a peal of Stedman Caters was rung by Guild members, composed and conducted by Washbrook. Blackbourn and Greenleaf were among the band, the latter strapping for Washbrook on the tenor. The account confirms that the peal was rung with the sanction of the Bath and Wells Diocesan Association "who were themselves unable to undertake the task with confidence."

A notice in *The Bell News* announced the event, and indicated that the invitation had been sent by the Dean and Chapter to the Master of the Oxford Guild, with the concurrence of the officers of the Bath and Wells Diocesan Association. The home guild felt they had insufficient experience of ten-bell ringing to undertake a peal. Incidentally a peal had to be rung, for the contract stated that the bell-hangers would not be paid until one was brought round.

One of the Wells ringers described the start of the ringing; the striking was as near perfection as possible and he hoped the local band would take note. At a meeting a few weeks later the local association officers were asked why the Oxford Guild had been invited to ring the peal. The Master of the Bath and Wells was prepared and read the correspondence between the officers and Robinson. The report does not quote it so we shall never know the details, but the members at that meeting unanimously passed a resolution deprecating the behaviour of the Master of the Oxford Diocesan Guild in the matter.

Nevertheless another invitation was extended to the Guild to ring a peal and in December 1894 Robinson and Coleridge accompanied Washbrook to the Cathedral. This time they rang John Cox's 5,021 Grandsire Caters singlehanded, with Washbrook conducting from the tenor. Four months later they achieved a peal of Kent Treble Bob Royal, Washbrook again conducting from the 57 cwt. tenor; it was the heaviest peal of Royal to be rung by only ten men. The day before leaving, they rang a peal of Double Norwich at St. Cuthbert's. One of the locals commented wryly that they might just as well take both rings of bells home with them, for no similar performances would be accomplished until they made another visit.

Within the Guild itself peals were growing in popularity and fresh ringers were constantly coming forward. In the Reading area there was a revival of interest, with one centre at Tilehurst, where J. Martin Routh, the chairman of the branch, lived. He was born in 1846, the son of the rector and a grand-nephew of the famous Dr. Martin Routh, president of Magdalen College. J.M.R., as he was known, was a well-liked figure, and after Oxford, he was called to the Bar. Whilst in Chambers in London he joined the College Youths and was Master in 1885. A fine handler himself, he was also a stickler for good striking, often terrifying careless ringers. During a cricket match he lost the sight of one eye when he was struck in the eye by a ball; subsequently this led to serious consequences for him at Lambourn. The opening peal after restoration was of Stedman Triples and he hit his good eye with his rope's end and went blind for a time.

He often related an amusing anecdote about the first peal at Tilehurst. After two and a half hours' ringing in the first attempt the tenor ringer gave up, and J.M.R. expressed his opinion of the poor chap in no uncertain manner. The leader of the old call change band asked him later if he could have rung the tenor himself for three hours, and he said that of course he could! The next time he went into the ringing room he rang the tenor and the call change conductor started moving the bells around and kept it up for three and a quarter hours! Then he congratulated J.M.R. on ringing the bell. The latter said he couldn't set the bell on the plea of dinner at the Rectory or any other excuse, without losing face. He could have cheerfully murdered the call-change man, who claimed to have called the first peal on the bells . . . J.M.R. was a great personality and although he did not ring many peals, he commanded much respect through his long life. He died in 1943, aged 96.

The first non-conducted peal for the Guild was at Tilehurst in 1892 when a Reading band rang Holt's Ten-Part of Grandsire Triples. Earlier they had rung the first peal of Bob Royal for the Guild at St. Lawrence's, Reading.

Across the river at nearby Caversham the band improved steadily. After the bells were augmented to eight in 1891 they rang 6,720 Double Norwich Court Bob Major within a year and within five years were regularly ringing peals of Stedman, Superlative, Cambridge and London. In 1900 they left the Guild after a disagreement and did not rejoin until 1908.

Members from the other three Reading towers made up a second peal band. In 1897 they attempted three peals in a day in three separate counties. First they rang a peal of Bob Major at St. Paul's, Wokingham, Berks; in the afternoon they rang Holt's Ten-Part at Hawley, Hants. Unfortunately in the evening they lost a peal of Treble Bob at Yorktown, Surrey. They were very disappointed about breaking down in the last course after two hours and fifty minutes good ringing.

Hughenden were the first band to secure a peal of London in the diocese, which John Evans conducted in December 1892. They followed on with two more in 1894 and another two the next year. They were thus some of the most advanced ringers in the country; only two other bands had scored more than one peal in the method. In Oxfordshire, Washbrook's band rang the first peal of London at St. Peter-in-the-East in 1893; Boyne Hill was the venue for the first in Berkshire in 1896.

In 1897 Robinson started a fund to augment the bells at Christ Church to a ring of twelve. Ten pounds was donated from Guild sources and the rest of the money was raised from the members. Two trebles were added and the sixth was recast, making the first ring of twelve in the Guild. The next year Washbrook called a peal of Kent Treble Bob Maximus, the first twelve bell peal to be rung in the diocese. It was rung half-muffled in memory of Lewis Carroll (Revd. C. L. Dodgson) who was a Fellow of Christ Church. Strangely, while the peal was in progress, Dr. Liddell, the father of "Alice" and one-time Dean of Christ Church, died.

Alice White, daughter of Henry White of Basingstoke, was the first woman to ring a tower bell peal in February 1896. Six months later she was invited to Tilehurst to ring a peal of Grandsire Triples, and so she became the first of her sex to ring a peal for the Guild. The first peal on the augmented bells at Hook Norton was of Stedman Triples, conducted by

Robinson. The tenor didn't go well, but its ringer had no difficulty. Unknown to the rest of the band, his brother was in the loft above the ringing chamber, helping!

The first peal of Stedman Cinques for the Guild was rung at Christ Church, composed and conducted by Washbrook, in January 1899. Later that year the first non-conducted peal of Stedman on tower bells was achieved for the Guild. This took place at Drayton on August Bank Holiday; an unsuccessful attempt lasting two hours preceded it.

A very fine performance was a peal of London Surprise Major at Merton College; here is Washbrook's account of this feat:

"However you have got the face to try ringing Major on Merton College bells is a knockout, and to try London Surprise by candlelight, too. What next, I wonder?'

'Look here, my boy, father has undertaken to erect the illuminations, and you can rest assured that it will be done satisfactorily.'

'All right, I shall come and listen to it. What time are you going to start?'

'Four o'clock, right off.'

This colloquy took place before the peal, recorded on another page, was rung. For the benefit of those who do not know Merton, it may be stated that the bells have to be rung from a gallery at an elevation of 56 feet from the tessellated floor of the chapel. This gallery is about three feet wide, and the ringers are protected from falling by an arrangement of wood and gas-piping. The chamber is 26 feet across, and the bells go very heavy and strike very false. Hence, we suppose, the above questioning.

Well, father arranged the candle business very nicely, for each ringer had one each side of him, and the light seemed pretty fair.

'Go-London' was called at 4.30 p.m., and all went very comfortable for about 1¼ hours, when it seemed evident that our candles were going much too fast, this caused some alarm, and was not productive of continued good ringing, however we meant going as far as the fat, 'both above and below,' would allow us, and we rolled them along well, again, for another hour; then matters looked very gloomy, for some of our illuminations had entirely disappeared, and it was very difficult to see whether the ringer opposite was pulling handstroke or backstroke; however, under the circumstances, we kept fairly good striking. Just at this time our good old friend 'Jimmy' could be heard aloft, replenishing the fat up there, which we down below felt very thankful for, and in a few minutes he appeared just inside the door of the ringing gallery with his electric bulls-eye.

By this time the faticles were hanging to our few remaining candles to an alarming extent. 'Fetch some more candles, Jimmy,' said a voice from the darkness. 'Right,' says Jimmy; and off he went across the chapel roof and down the stairs, and soon returned armed with two candles — all he could get, as the shops were closed.

These he lighted, and with considerable difficulty in getting along the gallery behind the ringers, managed to lighten our darkness on one side of the tower.

But it was soon evident that his services would be required the other side, for the Rev. and 'Old Tom' were getting very much clouded. 'Fetch some more, Jimmy,' is the cry. The much-wanted candles duly arrived, and just as 'Jimmy' arrived inside the door with them, the change 14235678 rolled up magnificently. No sooner had we entered upon this course, than the greatest difficulty of all presented itself, for by this time, although it was easy enough for the heavy bell men to see the light bell men, it was almost impossible for the latter to see the former, and together with the energy exhibited by 'Jimmy' in his endeavours to squeeze by the 5th and 6th men, and the sudden lighting of our darkness, no wonder that one or two of the band tripped about and spoilt the ringing of the last course, for ringing London Surprise under such trying circumstances would have been utterly impossible to any but cool-headed and careful ringers, and the band offer 'Jimmy' their best thanks, for, never was the services of a greaser more effectually realised; and it is certain that 8.10 would not have arrived so pleasantly had it not been for him."

(J. W. W., *The Bell News,* January 2nd, 1897).

Four record lengths were rung during the nineties. The first was 7,072 Superlative Surprise Major at Christchurch, Southgate. It was the longest length in the method but was later found to be false, so it cannot be counted.

On 31st December 1892 an attempt was made at Boyne Hill to ring the extent of Double Norwich with the tenors together. All went well for over five hours and then one of the band declared he could not carry on for the whole peal. Washbrook altered the composition and brought the bells round after 12,096 changes, rung in seven hours ten minutes. The ringers were: Revd. G. F. Coleridge, John Evans, W. H. L. Buckingham, Challis F. Winney, Herbert Baker, John W. Taylor, Revd. F. E. Robinson and James W. Washbrook. At the time it was the longest peal rung in the method.

In 1896 a band at Romford surpassed it with a peal of 13,440 changes. William Pye's band rang one of 15,072 changes at Erith in April 1899 and it was thought that this would remain the record for some time. However Washbrook had composed a longer length, and a month later, on Whit Monday, the following peal was rung:

KIDLINGTON, Oxford

On 22nd May, 1899, in 11 hours 12 minutes

17,042 DOUBLE NORWICH COURT BOB MAJOR

Harry G. Judge	Treble	William Bennett	5
Alfred E. Reeves	2	Frank Hopgood	6
Charles R. Lilley	3	Edwin Hims	7
John Tucker	4	James W. Washbrook	Tenor

Composed and conducted by J. W. Washbrook.

The greatest length rung in any method.

This peal aroused a tremendous furore in *The Bell News;* William Pye accused Washbrook of miscalling the peal and claimed that, as rung, it did not exceed the one he had called at Erith. The subsequent dispute was very acrimonious; intense rivalry caused unpleasant accusations to be made by people who should have known better. The matter was not resolved, so the record stood until 1904 when it was broken by a peal a few leads longer.

One record that did receive universal acclaim was 11,328 London Surprise Major at Drayton in 1896.

The record is as follows:

DRAYTON, Berks.

On 17th September, 1896, in 6 hours 6 minutes

11,328 LONDON SURPRISE MAJOR

Charles Hounslow	Treble	Edwin Hims	5
Frederick Exon	2	Thomas Payne	6
Charles H. Fowler	3	Revd. F. E. Robinson	7
Charles Exon	4	James W. Washbrook	Tenor

Composed and conducted by James W. Washbrook.

Charles Exon was only nineteen at the time: he wrote an account of the peal for *The Ringing World* when he was eighty-three.

The peal had finished about ten-thirty in the evening and Robinson invited them all to supper, saying they could go home in the morning. Someone suggested that they might just catch the last train from Abingdon to Oxford, so they hastened off to run the two miles to the station. It was pitch black and raining hard and Charlie Exon lost his way, only to arrive three minutes after the train had left! He then had no alternative but to walk the five miles into Oxford, despite having to rise at six the next morning to bake his bread.

Only about two hundred of the Guild members were involved in peal ringing; the remaining eighty-five per cent either could not, or would not ring peals. Oxfordshire was least represented. At the start of the decade, excluding the towers in Oxford itself, less than a fifth of the affiliated towers were in this county. Of the five branches the only one not wholly in Berkshire was the East Berks and South Bucks branch. This had enrolled more than two hundred members and was now almost the size of some of the smaller diocesan associations.

In 1892 two new branches were formed. The first, in the Chipping Norton deanery, was launched by Revd. C. S. Rowland, who became its first secretary and treasurer. Chipping Norton and Leafield were the two towers that joined; they had been affiliated for some time and the twenty-six members of the branch consisted of their ringers and one or two honorary members. The first meeting attracted ringers from Churchill and Shipton, but they were not tempted to join then.

The second branch founded that year was for North Buckinghamshire. Revd. J. H. Travers played an important part in its formation, drawing together the four towers already affiliated — Linslade, Stony

Stratford, Wing and Winslow — and persuading Emberton, Newton Longville and Olney to join. He became the first secretary and treasurer and did quite well with a membership of over fifty. Sadly the branch did not survive his move to Henley in 1894; six towers left the Guild and the branch collapsed, not to be revived until ten years later.

Three other branches made tentative beginnings during the decade but they all failed later on, either from lack of support or the presence of a strong personality to take charge. A Deddington Deanery branch was formed with great enthusiasm by W. Bradford from Bloxham, who was one of the Guild instructors. He became the first secretary and induced nine towers and seventy-two members to be affiliated. In 1896 the future looked bright for the branch but two years later the numbers had dropped to sixty-three and by 1900 they had fallen to forty-eight. By 1903 only eighteen members were left representing five towers: no subscriptions were collected and the branch soon ceased to exist.

The Henley Deanery branch was slightly more successful; it was begun in 1898 with fifty-two members from four towers. One of these was Caversham, who had ceded from the Reading branch, bringing with them sixteen members. The secretary was S. Goodall from Henley. In 1900 the numbers dropped to thirty-seven, mainly through Caversham retiring from the Guild. Henley took Newbury's place as the branch with the fewest members; it hovered around three dozen for some years, but it petered out in 1910.

For some years A. Thomas of Harwell had been agitating for the formation of a branch round the Drayton and Steventon area. Robinson was keen on the idea but reluctant to be involved as branch secretary. Finally an Abingdon ringer, G. Staniland, volunteered and the Abingdon branch came into being in 1900, with forty-nine ringers from six towers. These were the two Abingdon towers, Appleton, Hagbourne, Marcham and Radley; it is worth noting that neither Mr Thomas nor the Harwell band joined! Marcham left the following year and Radley two years after. Blewbury decided to join, but by then it was too late. The branch had no initiative left and it ceased to function in 1903.

Guild Rule ix stated that all members had to belong to the Church of England. This rule has not been applied now for nearly a quarter of a century, but eighty years ago it was a doctrine held with firm conviction by the clerical members and many of the educated laity. As each application for membership had to be supported by a testimonial from the parish priest, it might be thought that no problems would arise. In 1894, however, R. Buckingham from Great Marlow, applied to rejoin the Guild. He had left his tower and the Guild to join the Salvation Army, but later wished to go on with his ringing.

A special general meeting of the East Berks and South Bucks branch had to be called to consider his request. About twenty members turned up and listened to their chairman pronounce on the affair. He was very much against the re-admission of Buckingham, not for any personal reasons, but because it would lessen the authority of the Guild. People withdrawing their allegiance from the Church could not expect to be regarded as

Church Officers as the Rules envisaged. No one appeared to speak for the unfortunate man; he could not present his side of the case as he was not a member, so his application was rejected.

Hart-Davis proved to be a good successor to Dolben Paul in the administrative field. He had been involved in the formation of the Guild and at one branch meeting he said that the idea of the Guild had sprung from a paper he had presented on "Bells and Bell Ringing" at Dolben Paul's request. He was a competent organiser and the Annual General Meetings held at Woodstock, Wallingford, Chipping Norton and Wokingham in the years 1891-95 were very successful occasions.

The Woodstock meeting was the last at which over a quarter of the members were present. One of the items for discussion that day was a striking contest. William Newell proposed that certificates should be awarded to teams competing at branch annual meetings; a set of handbells could be awarded to the winning team which they would retain until the next contest. Some of the more austere clerical members thought this smacked of the bad old days of ringing matches, and would provoke rivalry and discontent. The proposition was eventually watered down to giving first, second or third class certificates to bands according to their merits. The Committee was instructed to consider the idea but no discussion ever took place.

The first grant from Guild funds towards the augmentation of a ring had gone to Holywell; as these bells were never increased to eight, the money was recovered and given to St. Peter-in-the-East. Shipton under Wychwood were made up from five to eight a few years later; the bells were hung directly on steel joists, without any additional bell-frame, probably one of the first occasions this method of hanging bells for change ringing was employed.

One of the problems facing the Committee when they organised the Festival at Long Crendon was the distance of the church from Thame Station. The two and a half mile walk each way was likely to be a deterrent to some people, but such fears were groundless and the day proved a great success.

Robinson made an unusual request at this meeting; he wanted the Guild to contribute a guinea towards the weighing of Christ Church tenor so that arguments about its weight could be settled. The Guild paid up! They also decided to hold three other quarterly meetings during the year: one was to be the Annual General Meeting of the East Berks and South Bucks branch and the remainder were to be held elsewhere in the Guild. They did not prove successful; only twenty-two members attended the meetings held at Woodstock and Wantage. They were discontinued a few years later.

The last five Annual General Meetings of the century were held at Bletchley, Banbury, Maidenhead, High Wycombe and Oxford. At the Bletchley meeting in 1896 Hart-Davis announced his retirement as secretary at the end of the year as the work involved was proving too much for him. He was persuaded to stay on and Arthur W. Pike of Reading was appointed to help him with certificates and applications for membership.

He was given the title of Assistant Honorary Secretary and the report records that it was a "very public-spirited act on the part of a working man" to accept the post.

Throughout the country there was great rejoicing for the Diamond Jubilee of Queen Victoria, and a number of rings of bells in the diocese were augmented to mark the occasion. Three towers applied for grants for this kind of work; Beedon and Kimble each received three guineas as a contribution towards the costs of their augmentations from four to six, and Kidlington received five pounds for unspecified improvements.

At High Wycombe in 1899 Hart-Davis again claimed that his workload was too heavy and the Minutes record his retirement as Secretary. Appointed in his place was A. H. Cocks, author of *Church Bells of Buckinghamshire*. The Minutes for the next Annual Meeting however show that Hart-Davis was again elected Secretary and Treasurer and that Cocks was Guild Festival Secretary, an arrangement which continued for the next three years. It appears that Cocks was only willing to undertake part of the Secretary's job; he had wanted to appoint three assistants to help. In the end he backed down and left Hart-Davis to do all the work.

After the luncheon at High Wycombe Robinson was presented with some splendid gifts. The first was an elegant, solid silver salad bowl in an old Irish pattern; engraved on it were the details of his most notable peals, and it carried the following inscription:

"Presented to the Rev. F. E. Robinson, Master of the Oxford Diocesan Guild of Bellringers since its institution in 1881, during the 19th year of his Mastership, in appreciation of his great services, by many members of the Guild. — July 17th, 1899."

In addition he received a small Queen Anne silver tea set with an unusually large tea pot, and an illuminated address which was in book form, bound in morocco and engrossed and illuminated on vellum. Emblazoned inside were the twelve peals that Robinson regarded as his finest achievements, as well as the names of the six hundred Guild members who had contributed to the gift. The first page carried this dedication:

"To the Rev. F. E. Robinson, MA, Master of the Oxford Diocesan Guild of Church Bell Ringers.

Rev. and Dear Sir,

We, the undersigned, honorary and ringing members of the Guild, in asking your acceptance of the accompanying gift, desire to assure you of our grateful and heartfelt appreciation of the services you have rendered the Guild as its Master from the day of its institution in 1881 to the present time. The high place taken by the Guild among similar institutions in this country, and the sound churchmanship and scientific efficiency of its change ringing members, are sufficient and satisfactory testimony to the value of your work. Many church bells and belfries in this diocese have been improved or restored by your helpful and ever-ready counsels. It is our earnest hope that you may be spared in full health and strength for many more years of office and untiring and zealous activity, and that God may bless and prosper your work in the future as abundantly as in the past."

The address was illuminated by Arthur W. Pike, the Assistant Secretary, and examples of his fine lettering can be seen today in belfries in the Reading area. According to the account, Robinson was taken aback at the gifts. But he rallied and paid tribute to his wife for her encouragement and said that Washbrook's ability and skill had enabled him to ring more peals than any other man. It is a pity that these gifts have not survived.

The dawn of the new century saw the Guild entering a new phase of its own existence. Some of the old stalwarts had died: Revd. S. F. Marshall, rector of Farnham Royal for thirty-seven years and one of the founders of the East Berks and South Bucks Society, as well as the Guild, died during the '90s aged seventy-five. Jesse Avery who had stood in the long peals at Appleton in 1888, died from consumption. Charles Swain of Newbury and J. C. Truss Snr. of Marlow, both of whom were active in their respective branches, also died.

Finally the Guild lost the services of the best known ringer in the country. James Washbrook moved to Arklow in Ireland to take up the post of verger and ringing instructor at the new church Lord Carysfort had built on his estate. Had this happened ten years earlier, the fortunes of the Guild might have taken a different turn. As it was, the Guild had enjoyed the benefits of his genius for everything connected with ringing for the whole of its life. When he left, other men had been encouraged by his example and enthusiasm, and were ready to carry the Guild forward into the new age.

Chapter Nine

CONSOLIDATION

The ringing-in of the new century at Bradfield, Berks. typifies some of the changes that were to sweep over the Guild within the next few years. The foreman, T. D. Rowe, had taught a number of women to ring there, and six of them rang in the opening touch of 1900.

The first woman to ring a peal was Mrs George Williams, who rang one of Grandsire Triples on handbells in 1892. Alice White, as we noted in an earlier chapter, rang the first on tower bells in 1896, and it may have been the peal she rang later that year at nearby Tilehurst which suggested this new source of recruits to Rowe. The best member of the band was Mary Chillingworth. Born in 1882, one of the daughters of a local farmer, she quickly became an accomplished ringer and took part in a number of peals before the First World War. In 1907 she joined the Ancient Society of College Youths, one of the handful of women ever to be elected. Five years later she took over the captaincy of the tower and managed it skilfully until her marriage in 1916. She became the second wife of the Guild

General Secretary, Albert E. Reeves; the marriage ceremony was performed by the Guild Master, Rev. C. W. O. Jenkyn. After the wedding, she conducted a 720 of Bob Minor — it was the first time a bride had called her own "wedding peal".

Up to the period of the War, there were very few women members of the Guild. It is difficult to be certain, for their names appear in the Report with initials only, exactly like the men. A motion passed at the East Berks and South Bucks meeting in 1908 changed this; their four new lady members from Lane End were to have "Miss" printed in front of their names. In some areas women were not even allowed to appear as members of a tower. Eva N. Belcher, of Shipton-under-Wychwood, rang several peals of Stedman Triples, but local pressure forced the inclusion of her name under the list of unattached members of the Chipping Norton branch. Kathleen Holifield, daughter of the tower captain at Abingdon, also had her name entered as an unattached member, but nearby Blewbury were proud to include their peal ringing Miss M. W. Nightingale as a member of the tower. There were also lady ringers at Cookham, Bucklebury, Mapledurham, St. Giles Reading, Aston Tirrold, South Stoke, and Goring.

The Guild continued to increase in numbers. In 1901 the total membership was 1,357 and by 1914, it was 1,976. Several new branches had been created while those at Abingdon, Deddington and Henley fell by the wayside. The Witney area had been fortunate to secure the services of Revd. C. W. O. Jenkyn, an energetic young man, recently down from Cambridge. He served his first curacy at Waltham St. Lawrence, but from 1899 to 1910 he was at Witney, where he provided the spur needed to form a new branch. In 1902 he brought together the sixty-six ringers from the towers of Burford, Ducklington, Freeland, Kidlington, Stanton Harcourt, Witney, Woodstock and Yarnton to make up a Witney and Woodstock branch.

Two years later, on 11th June 1904, the North Bucks branch was founded at a meeting at Newton Longville, where the Vicar, Revd. C. L. Norris, provided the impetus. He became the first chairman and A. E. Powell the first secretary. They persuaded one hundred and thirty-five members to join from sixteen towers, fifteen of these joining or rejoining the Guild. Their excellent work continued and during the next few years they encouraged eleven more towers to join and raised the membership to over two hundred and fifty.

By the time George V came to the throne, there were eight branches and the largest was still the East Berks and South Bucks with 336 members. North Bucks followed with about a hundred fewer and Chipping Norton was third with 175. Newbury was the only one with less than a hundred members.

In 1913 two more branches were established; the first was in the Vale of the White Horse, an area almost destitute of change ringers. Revd. R. C. L. Newhouse, Vicar of Buckland, was the instigator; he was the son of Revd. R. P. Newhouse, one of the first secretaries of the East Berks and South Bucks branch and by this time rural dean of Reading. The five towers constituting the new branch were Buckland, Coleshill, Hinton

Waldrist, Longcot and Longworth. Of the forty-three members, only three joined as change ringers; the remainder could only manage rounds and call-changes.

The other branch was based on the district around Bicester, and Edwin Hims, a talented protege of Washbrook, became its first secretary. The forty-seven members came from Bicester, Middleton Stoney, Somerton, Islip, and Launton, the last two joining the Guild for the first time.

Both these branches made slow progress, and probably because they are less well populated areas, they have never achieved the membership of the other branches with similar numbers of towers.

It was the custom when a new branch was established to hold the Guild Annual General Meeting there in the following year. Witney was visited in 1903 and Bletchley in 1905. An attempt was made to revive the flagging Henley branch by going there in 1906: the next year they went to Abingdon.

Meetings were not so lengthy in those days; perhaps fewer people were articulate, but the attendance was certainly greater than at meetings during the 1960s. Many of the items on the agenda are familiar today — the subscription, the cost of the Report, payment of grants and so on. An unusual motion appeared in 1901: "to grant free life membership to all those who had served, or were still serving with the colours in South Africa."

An item which caused controversy later on was the payment of £20 each year to Robinson for his personal expenses, the Guild Committee noting that he was excessively generous in paying the expenses of his peal ringing colleagues. In 1904 the committee of the East Berks and South Bucks branch objected to this grant. Later in the year, at their own branch meeting, Robinson said that he rarely claimed the allowance; in any event, he declined to sink into the position of a mere instructor. He said that he preferred to ring peals of Stedman, but would be willing to ring peals in other methods if satisfactory bands could be assembled.

Robinson's habit of ringing a peal before the Guild A.G.M. did not meet with universal approval. His 997th peal was rung on the morning of the Bletchley meeting in 1905. Later that year the branch passed a resolution that no touch of more than fifteen minutes' duration should be rung before a meeting.

Despite some grumbling in the provinces, he had many friends and his 1,000th peal was the subject of much rejoicing. It was attempted at Drayton on 7th August 1905 and was intended to be a repetition of the silent peal rung six years earlier. Washbrook returned from Ireland to participate, and rang 3-4. A mistake in the Slow work caused a breakdown after three parts, so a second attempt was made with Robinson conducting. This was brought to an end by a broken rope after two hours' ringing. Two days later the peal was rung with this band:

DRAYTON, Berks.
On 9th August, 1905, in 2 hours 47 minutes.
5040 STEDMAN TRIPLES

J. W. Washbrook Jnr.	Treble	C. H. Fowler	5
G. A. Smith	2	H. Miles	6
F. Hopgood	3	Revd. F. E. Robinson	7
J. W. Washbrook	4	Revd. G. F. Coleridge	Tenor

Conducted by Revd. F. E. Robinson

This was the first time anyone had rung a thousand peals and Robinson was showered with congratulations. After the 1906 Central Council meeting Sir Arthur Heywood gave a magnificent banquet for him at the Westminster Palace Hotel.

All the attention made him more single-minded in the pursuit of his second ambition — a thousand peals of Stedman Triples. He clashed with Plain Speaker in *The Bell News*, who commented that he ought not to ring eight bell peals in ten and twelve bell towers. Robinson retorted that there was no reason why he should not prefer to ring peals of Stedman Triples. Some of his exploits may have damaged the Exercise generally; he rang a peal at Tetbury, Glos. under some difficulties. The vicar and sexton "invaded" the belfry and tried to stop the ringing! On a number of occasions he lost peals because people stood their bells rather than be "put right". Perhaps some ringers could not tolerate his personal habits during peals. William Welling, then a young man, rang a dozen or so peals with Robinson towards the end of his ringing career, and he recorded that Robinson used to fill his mouth with raisins at the start of a peal and spit all the pips out at intervals. If the peal was successful he would say: "Thank you gentlemen, for your careful ringing," and intone a prayer. If the attempt failed, he would don his coat and leave, without a word.

He was not entirely fit; he tried to resign from the Mastership in 1901, and again in 1905 after a serious operation. Each time, however, he bowed to pressure from the Committee and stood again. He suffered a further severe illness in 1908 which forced him to miss the Annual General Meeting for the first time. After his recovery, he moved to Wokingham where he spent his remaining months. He rang a few more peals and died on 10th February, 1910, aged seventy-seven.

Ringing was not his only hobby. He was a skilful wood-carver, and during his time at Drayton, had carved the organ-case, the choir stalls and bench-ends. He started on a chancel screen but died before making much progress. It was decided to try to raise £320 to complete it; unfortunately, despite sending out 5,000 copies of the appeal, only £195 was subscribed. A smaller screen was erected across the tower arch and memorial tablets were placed in the church, as well as at Appleton and in the cloisters of Christ Church, Oxford.

Fortunately for the Guild a new man was ready to take over as Master. The Revd. C. W. O. Jenkyn was elected Deputy Master in 1905 and quickly established himself as a worthy successor. He was born at East Garston, Berks, in 1874 and his father was the rector there. Although he learned to ring at home, he had no experience of change ringing until he went up to Cambridge. His first peal was Holt's Ten-Part in 1894; it was also the first tower bell peal for the Cambridge University Guild. He became an accomplished heavy bell ringer and rang the tenors at Bow and Southwark to peals. During his curacy at Witney he assisted in the formation of a good change ringing band; unlike Robinson, he took a great interest in teaching. He insisted on good ringing, and retained a preference for well-struck rounds to badly executed changes. In his youth he had been a fine oarsman and he continued to be passionately interested in rowing. He was a member of the exclusive Leander Club and frequently helped at Henley Regatta.

The General Secretary was still Revd. R. H. Hart-Davis, who was assisted by Arthur W. Pike from 1896 to 1902, when Albert E. Reeves took over. After nine years as understudy he succeeded Hart-Davis in 1911. His apprenticeship had been hard; Hart-Davis wanted to resign in 1903 and was only persuaded to continue if an assistant was found who would do nearly all the work. Reeves was a working man so the Committee decided he should be paid for his efforts and the sum of £12 was allocated to him. It was increased to £15 in 1905 and to £20 in 1910.

In recognition of his valuable administrative work during his twenty-one years in the office of secretary, Hart-Davis was presented with a leather armchair and a silver inkstand. He went on with the job of Treasurer until 1923, when he retired to make way for a younger man.

The Report for 1908 carried for the first time a now familiar name: Ernest Francis was elected auditor and he and his successors have carried out this task ever since.

In those days members expressed their thanks to retiring officers in more tangible ways. Pike was presented with a smoker's cabinet in oak and Reeves was given a barometer by a grateful band he had taught at Sonning. The North Bucks branch seemed particularly fond of inscribed silver inkstands — they presented three to retiring officers, all within six years!

Several significant changes to the Rules were made. A Reserve Fund was set up in 1905 and life members' and non-resident life members' subscriptions were channelled into it. The next rule change concerned the post of Master. In 1911, the year after Jenkyn took office, it was decided that the post should only be held by a change ringer. The Minute book gives no indications or reasons why; it doesn't even record the names of those responsible for the motion. Lastly, agitation from some of the smaller branches showed that their representation on the Guild Committee was inadequate. In 1914, one representative for every fifty branch members was allowed, and the secretary and chairman of each branch were ex-officio members. It was also decided that women could become committee members, and Mary Chillingworth was the first so to serve.

Other subjects debated at length included the crediting of peals to branches, and the inclusion of practice nights and the weights of tenors in the Report. The last were not adopted; in 1910 they agreed to add just the foreman's address. A sub-committee was set up to consider a service book which was debated for three years and produced finally by S. P. C. K. in 1914. In 1906 the North Bucks branch had prepared a service sheet in far less time!

Revd. H. C. Wilder was rector of Farnham Royal, succeeding Revd. S. F. Marshall. His close association with J. J. Parker made him enthusiastic about ringing and he was secretary of the East Berks and South Bucks branch for some years. He moved to Sulham in 1909 and while there wrote the hymn "Unchanging God who livest", which was probably sung at the 1912 festival for the first time.

In 1913 a proposal was put forward for a Guild badge and it was left to the Committee to design one. As the Central Council was considering a national ringer's badge, they deferred taking any action and nothing was done. The division of the Guild into three archdeaconries was discussed: nothing was done.

Holding the Annual General Meeting and Festival at different places each year came in for some criticism, especially from the North Bucks branch, who found it impossible to reach some parts of Berkshire by train unless they set out the day before the meeting! They suggested that it should always be held in Oxford, which was strongly resisted by the powerful Berkshire contingents. They were successful in blocking this change until the 1920s when some angry scenes enlivened the Annual General Meetings.

The wartime meetings were mainly concerned with keeping the Guild running when many of the members were serving at the front. The names of those serving were to be kept in the list of members without any further subscriptions, which seemed the least they could do. Those who were left behind were asked to pay an extra sixpence on their subscriptions to ensure the Guild's solvency.

The Master was serving in France as an Army Chaplain and won the M.C. for bringing in wounded men under fire on the notorious Ypres Salient. In his absence the Committee decided that the Guild ought to have some trustees and A. J. Wright, Revd. R. H. Ackworth and Revd. G. F. Coleridge were selected. One of their first jobs was the purchase of a fireproof safe in which to keep the Guild records and property.

At a Reading branch meeting in 1916 one of the Central Council representatives — probably Frank Hopgood — was asked to give a report. He said that the Council had done nothing and the whole meeting had been a farce. This sparked off an argument at the Guild Annual General Meeting later that year when a motion that the Guild should withdraw from the Council was debated fiercely. After an eloquent speech by Coleridge the motion was lost.

Let us now look at some of the ringing that took place in the first decade of the twentieth century. The majority of the peals were, of course, Stedman Triples, with Robinson as conductor. He always called a variation of Thurstan's peal; other conductors were less conservative. F. Boreham called Carter's Odd Bob One-Part and T. H. Taffender several other one-part compositions. Local bands rang peals at Streatley and Compton, both of which were the first for all the ringers. Stedman Cinques at Christ Church was the first by an all local band, although this might be disputed since Robinson conducted it. In 1904 the North Bucks branch rang their first peal — Grandsire Doubles at Newton Longville. Later on they scored Bob Major at Olney. The first peal of Triples by members of the Sonning Deanery branch was rung in 1905.

The band at Boyne Hill made good progress, mainly due to the skill of a young man called George Martin. Born in 1877 he took up ringing when he was sixteen and called his first peal two years later. This was Grandsire Triples, achieved at the fiftieth attempt! He was a very reliable ringer, an excellent striker and a brilliant conductor. He was also a first-rate instructor and with his help the local band rang peals of Kent, Double Norwich, Superlative, Cambridge and London. His friends were so pleased with their success that they gave him a marble clock in appreciation of his helping them to ring more advanced methods. He was kindly, though outspoken, and held in high esteem by all who knew him.

Excellent bands existed at Caversham and Hughenden. The former rejoined the Guild in 1908 and were soon recording peals of Cambridge, London and Superlative; Bristol followed in 1912. At Hughenden the first peal of Forward Major was rung for the Guild in 1910.

Another good conductor was G. F. Williams of High Wycombe, and he called the first peal of Erin Triples for the Guild at Wooburn in 1911. In 1912 he called nineteen peals including London and Bristol Major, Erin Caters and Kent Maximus. Another, of Stedman Caters at High Wycombe, was by an entirely local band. A record one hundred and twenty-two peals were rung that year, including one of Minor, lamenting the loss of the Titanic.

For some reason the number of peals slumped by a third in 1913. The leading conductor was George Martin who called eleven. The Caversham band demonstrated their prowess by ringing the first ever peal in a Surprise Principle, which was one of Washbrook's creations. It was entitled "Washbrook's Surprise Principle", although it was published with the more mundane name of "Caversham Major". Another first for the Guild was a peal of Stedman Caters on handbells, rung at Guildford and conducted by Alfred H. Pulling.

After the outbreak of War in August 1914, the Master expressed a wish that peals should not be rung until hostilities had ceased. Only one further peal was rung that year, half-muffled in memory of the Bishop of Buckingham's son. Twenty peals were rung during the next four years, most of them to mark some specific occasion.

Over eight hundred men from the Guild served in the Forces during the war and five women members enrolled as nurses. A total of one hundred and nineteen died; the first member to be killed in action was G. Bedford from Theale.

The Guild lost several well-known ringers. William Bennett, of the bell-hanging firm of Webb and Bennett, Kidlington, died in November 1903. He was a very experienced ringer and had taken part in the record peals in 1888 and also the long peal at Kidlington. Harry Judge, another man from this tower and a relative of Walter F. Judge, died a few years later.

Redan Sear of Bletchley was the eldest son of Thomas Sear, tower captain at Bletchley from 1861-1880. Redan succeeded him and held the post until his own death in 1906, aged forty-five. His family was the mainstay of ringing in that part of the county for over a century.

In 1910 James R. Haworth died. Although he had not been a resident member, he had acted as an instructor in the early days, especially in the Sonning Deanery branch. A contemporary of his was Charlie Hounslow, who was born in Oxford on 10th February, 1832. He became a painter and signwriter by trade and his work can be seen in many belfries throughout the diocese; his best peal board is in St. Lawrence's, Reading. He was popular amongst ringers and was described as "one of Nature's gentlemen." In his younger days he would walk many miles for a short touch of Grandsire or Stedman. An excellent striker, he was invited in several long peals, including the 15,041 Stedman Caters in 1888 and the 11,328 London Surprise Major at Drayton. He didn't keep a complete record of his peals but the Reports show that he rang a hundred and seventy-one, mostly with Washbrook. In 1881 he called the Guild's first peal at Kirtlington. He died on 15th March, 1913, aged eighty-one.

A number of new rings of bells were installed in 1913, amongst them Bicester, Slough, Twyford and Warfield. Over the period covered by this chapter, eighteen towers received grants from the General Fund totalling £53 5s. The church, tower and bells at Wargrave were destroyed by an act of arson on 1st June 1914 — the work of Suffragettes. A new ring of eight was placed in the rebuilt church two years later.

This Chapter began by relating how the first women joined the Guild. Throughout the Edwardian era, their numbers slowly increased and some of them were skilful ringers. In 1905, Mary Chillingworth was the first resident lady ringer to score a peal for the Guild. Throughout the Edwardian era, their numbers slowly increased and some of them were skilful ringers.

This Chapter began by relating how the first women joined the Guild. Throughout the Edwardian era, their numbers slowly increased and some of them were skilful ringers. In 1905, Mary Chillingworth was the first resident lady ringer to score a peal for the Guild. Mary Nightingale rang a peal of Grandsire Triples in 1910; Ethel Goodship, Eva Belcher and Kathleen Holifield all rang peals in 1913.

With over half the male ringers at the front, many more women were recruited. Hurst had seven under their own foreman, Miss Roe. The twelve male members — of whom nine were in France — were under the leadership of Joseph White!

The arrival of women in the belfry was greeted by suspicion by some of the older Victorian ringers, especially the clergy. It was probably they who insisted on the passing of the following resolution at the 1915 General Committee Meeting:

"The Committee of the Oxford Diocesan Guild feels that the rule of the Church must be observed with regard to the covering of a woman's head in the belfry while ringing. The Ladies' Guild be asked to devise some suitable covering that can, if necessary, be substituted for the hat."

In view of the size of Edwardian picture hats, perhaps it was a wise move to seek something smaller!

Chapter Ten

THE TWENTIES

The Armistice brought to an end one of bloodiest conflicts known to man, and ringing, like other occupations and hobbies, tried to return to its pre-war level of competence. Although standards could be exceeded, the past could not be re-created, and the 1920s were vastly different from the period before the War. Nearly half the Guild had been wrenched from their usual placid existence and plunged into the maelstrom of the trenches. They returned, hoping for a better world, but did not find it.

In 1919 the membership was still artificially inflated due to the inclusion of those who had served through the War. Many did not return to ringing and it was the end of the next decade before the total membership exceeded that of 1914.

The East Berks and South Bucks branch seemed to be an exception. At their meeting in April 1920, William Fussell, their secretary, proudly announced that they had more than six hundred members – over a quarter of the Guild total! Four hundred and seventy-four were resident ringing members; eleven were clergymen and forty-three were women. Their list of honorary members was sixty-eight and they had enrolled eighty-four non-resident life members.

All these people were very proud that their branch was established as a separate entity two years before the Guild. Besides the largest membership, the branch covered the biggest area and contained the most competent ringers. Peals of Surprise were frequently attempted, and often scored. At High Wycombe, the twelve bells could be rung to Stedman Cinques and Kent Treble Bob Maximus. From all viewpoints the branch was pre-eminent and it was hard for the members to realise that they could not dictate to the Guild.

Before the War the North Bucks branch had tried unsuccessfully to persuade the Guild to hold the Festival and Annual General Meeting in Oxford every year. Jenkyn was in favour, for he considered the Cathedral the centre of the diocese and holding a service there each year would forge a closer link with the Church. The members of the East Berks and South Bucks branch did not agree. They thought it was unfair to hold the Annual General Meeting in Oxfordshire each time; it should rotate round the three arch-deaconries or alternate between Reading and Oxford.

In 1919 it was at Oxford and in 1920 at Reading, with the result that the attendance was halved and four of the thirteen branches were not represented. The next three Festivals took place in Oxford, which provoked the East Berks and South Bucks branch to pass the following resolution at their meeting in 1922:

"We view with alarm the decision to hold the Festival yet again at Oxford, for we believe that it is contrary to the best interests of the Guild to hold it in one centre."

They suggested that a referendum be taken of all towers in union with the Guild.

No notice appears to have been taken of these suggestions, so the next year several towers withdrew their membership. Feeling ran very high in the branch and many subscriptions were withheld. The Guild officers were in a difficult position and Jenkyn was disheartened by the whole affair. He commented in the Report that decisions were made by the members attending the Annual General Meeting, and not by any one individual or any one branch.

The decision was taken at the 1923 Festival to hold it at Oxford again the following year. It may have been an attempt to mollify the dissidents that led the officers to switch it to Reading; they reported that Oxford was not available "owing to unavoidable circumstances." All future Festivals were held in Oxford, despite arguments to the contrary every year. Some of the towers who had left, rejoined the Guild soon after, but High Wycombe, from where most of the strong opposition had come, did not affiliate itself again for a quarter of a century.

Billy Fussell was a very astute man and probably foresaw many of the problems that were going to arise in his area; he retired from the office of branch secretary in 1922. His successor tried to cope, but proved unequal to the task. It was not until Arthur D. Barker was appointed in 1924 that the branch began to grow in stature again.

Five new branches were established in the 1920s. The first was the North Berkshire branch which finally came into being on 4th December 1920. Fourteen towers, with one hundred and thirty-three members joined; their first chairman was the Revd. P. P. Goldingham and the first secretary, H. R. Cooper. He only remained in office for six months and then Albert E. Lock took over. For the next forty years he guided the branch and built it into the viable unit it is today.

Albert Lock came from Sutton Courtenay, where his family had owned "The Plough" for several generations. He was born in 1879 and, after his schooldays, followed other members of his family into their 150 year old monumental mason's business. He was a master craftsman; his work includes the memorial tablets to Jenkyn and Coleridge in the cloisters at Christ Church. He had wide-ranging interests and played cricket for Berkshire, besides being a good footballer and a fine fisherman.

He learned to ring in his boyhood home – going into the ground-floor belfry with other lads of his own age and ringing the bells half up. They used to leave the ropes swinging and dash away as the ringers approached!

Eventually he taught himself to ring and became captain of the band. He acquired his change ringing with Revd. F. E. Robinson, who called his first peal in 1906 – Stedman Triples, of course! In all he rang about 225 peals, mostly with his wife, Kathleen, whom he married in 1916.

She was the daughter of Henry Holifield, of the famous Appleton family. In 1908, when she was twenty-two, she learned to ring, and rang regularly with her father and brother at Abingdon, although they would not let her join the band! Her first peal was in 1913 and altogether she rang 162, on all numbers of bells and in most of the standard methods.

The South Oxon and Mid-Bucks branch was formed at Great Milton in November 1921. The vicar there, the Revd. J. T. Fox was a ringer and Jenkyn persuaded him to invite ringers from many of the nearby towers to an inaugural meeting. Support was given by the presence of the Guild officers and Billy Fussell, who may have done some teaching there earlier on. Twelve towers joined in the first year, including five who were affiliated for the first time. Seventy members were enrolled and Fox became the first chairman, with P. Wilson, the Warborough schoolmaster as secretary.

On 15th June 1922 an Oxford and District branch came into being – this time to stay! The Guild officers were present and witnessed the election of Revd. C. C. Inge, vicar of St. Giles, as chairman and W. Harris as a non-ringing secretary. He gave up the post in the following year and his place was taken by A. F. Barrett, foreman at St. Aldate's. The Report shows that eight towers and fifty-eight members comprised the branch.

About this time Maurice Smith of Banbury convinced many of the local ringers that a branch of the Guild was necessary in the northern part of Oxfordshire, and in June 1925 the Banbury and District branch was formed. The first chairman was the vicar of Adderbury, Revd. C. F. Cholmondley and R. R. Lewis of Banbury was the secretary. The towers of Adderbury, Banbury, Cropredy, Deddington, Great Tew, Warmington and Wardington joined; there were eleven honorary members and forty-three ringing members.

The only remaining area which was not adequately covered was in Central Buckinghamshire; there was no natural centre and change ringing was virtually non-existent. Long Crendon had seen spasms of activity, but the district awaited the right man to lead it – he was Revd. J. F. Amies. He was a competent ringer and tutor and had been an enthusiastic member of the East Berks and South Bucks branch whilst he was vicar of Chalfont St. Giles. When he was appointed rector of the three-bell tower at Edgcote, he found himself in territory indifferent to change ringing. Undeterred, he cycled out to local towers three or four nights each week, encouraging young churchmen to take up the Art, and ignoring the apathy of the call-change ringers. Commencing on 23rd June, 1926, he held a series of half-day meetings and practices. Although to start with, they could only manage rounds and call-changes, they soon progressed to Grandsire, Stedman, and Plain Bob.

The new branch was formed at a meeting at Granborough on 18th

February 1928; ringers from eleven towers were present, as well as the Master, Secretary and Treasurer of the Guild. The company took only a few minutes to decide to form a branch, but finding a name for it proved more time consuming. Finally, the new chairman, Revd. G. Dixon, suggested it should be the Central Bucks branch, which was accepted. Amies was the first secretary and treasurer. Strangely; there is no mention of the founding of this branch in the Report – it simply appears from nowhere!

The first two items considered after the War were the subscription and a War memorial. The subscription had remained unchanged since the inaugural meeting of 1881; post-war costs forced an increased of 50 per cent, from 1s 0d to 1s 6d! The memorial took the form of a tablet in the cloisters at Christ Church and a book containing the names of the fallen. The work cost £58 10s and a further 11s 0d was spent on hiring buglers for the dedication service.

There was much contention during the twenties. Some good suggestions were made at meetings, but most of them were hammered! For instance, the idea of a Guild badge was revived, and dropped. It was suggested that a copy of the Rules, with a fly-leaf front page for a membership certificate should be produced and this too was rejected. Alterations to the Report format, such as one-line peal reports with a *Ringing World* reference, a peal fee of 3d per rope, and the inclusion of ringing times, were all thrown out. Even the sensible idea of a sub-committee first considering the applications for grants was rebuffed. Conversely, some potentially controversial matters were readily accepted. In 1923 some Rules revisions were proposed, which went through without amendment, question or discussion!

One of these new rules created the post of Vice-President for those performing meritorious service for the Guild. Revd. R. H. Hart-Davis retired from the treasurership in 1923 and Arthur J. Wright, a non-ringer from Reading, took his place. In recognition of Hart-Davis' work for the Guild in the forty-two years since its foundation, he was elected a Vice-President in 1925. In 1926 two more men received this honour. Revd. A. C. R. Freeborn had been chairman of the Witney and Woodstock branch since its formation, and a keen friend to ringers for over forty years. W. Pole Routh had been an active ringer in his youth and had been chairman of the Reading branch for seventeen years.

Three more men were singled out in this way during the decade. Canon Coleridge was a popular and well-known figure throughout the diocese and had been elected President of the Central Council in 1921. The Guild honoured him by making him a Vice-President in 1927. J. J. Parker was perhaps the best known lay ringer in the Guild at that time and was also elected. The last recipient of this distinction was the Revd. Dr. T. Archer-Houblon, at one time Archdeacon of Oxford, who was elected in 1929.

Hart-Davis died in 1928 and was greatly missed. Although he was not a practical ringer, he always had the welfare of ringers and the success of the guild at heart. His daughter presented his set of thirteen handbells to the Master for the use of any tower in the Guild. Since then they have been restored twice and are in the care of the Deputy Master.

The decade started with the deaths of two well-known North Bucks ringers. Valentine Sear, the younger son of Thomas Sear, died in 1920 and his three sons, Harry, Walter and Fred, carried on the family tradition at Bletchley. C. A. Valentine of Stony Stratford, whilst still a young man, died of pneumonia in 1920. He had been a driving force in peal ringing in that area and, had he lived, would have become well-known throughout the Guild.

On Christmas Day 1923 James W. Washbrook died in Manchester. He had not lived in the diocese for more than a generation, but such was his charisma that his death was felt keenly by many who had never met him. His sons had left Ireland to find work in the Manchester area, and he followed about 1911. He rang at St. Thomas, Pendleton, with his son J. W. Washbrook, Jnr.; three of his other sons were killed in the War.

A committee was elected to consider the form of his memorial. The addition of two bells to one of the sixes in Oxford seemed an obvious choice, and estimates were obtained from Whites, and Mears and Stainbank for augmenting St. Ebbe's or St. Giles. It was decided to proceed with the former and an appeal was made in *The Ringing World* for a minimum of £160. The final amount raised was £238 3s 4d, of which £209 13s 8d was spent on retuning, rehanging and augmenting, as well as placing a bronze tablet in the ringing chamber. The remaining money was invested to provide maintenance of the bells and ropes at St. Ebbe's.

The dedication was on 5th December 1925, performed by Canon Coleridge. Written invitations were sent to all the subscribers, and Guild members donated the tea. The tablet is inscribed:

ANNO DOMINI 1925

The bells in this tower were repaired and rehung and two trebles added by the Oxford Diocesan Guild and ringers of the British Empire in memory of

JAMES W. WASHBROOK

a highly skilled ringer, a talented composer, and an able conductor, for many years instructor to the Guild.

Born July 27, 1864

Died Christmas Day 1923

Several other notable members died in the twenties. William Newell, "the father of ringing in Reading", died in January 1924, aged 85. Revd. E. Broome, for many years the secretary of the Sonning Deanery branch, died in the same year. In 1927 Frederick Webb died; he was the head of the bell-hanging firm of Webb and Bennett at Kidlington, and his work can be seen throughout the diocese. He was a reliable and sincere man of few words, who served for a long time on the Guild General Committee. A. H. Cocks, one-time Festival Secretary, died in 1929.

The ten years after the end of the War were intensely busy for the bell-founders. Restorations, rehangings and augmentations proved to be ideal War memorials and in subsquent years the growing ambitions of bands led to many more rings being increased to six, eight or ten. Thirty-five towers applied for grants, and £123 was paid out. There was so much activity on this front that the new Treasurer introduced a Restoration Fund in 1926, although in its first year it only grew to £3 5s!

Jenkyn had continued Robinson's practice of visiting towers and making recommendations on the work to be carried out. These comments on some of the results of his recommendations appear in the 1929 Report:

"Of the other towers, there are four in which may be found excellent examples of what can be done by careful modern tuning. Newbury and St. Lawrence, Reading, are as good as many of us believed they might be; St. Mary's, Reading, are a great deal better than most of us thought possible; Thatcham with two trebles added are a surprise even to the founders themselves."

In 1929 he and Tom Hibbert started a fund to have St. Lawrence, Reading augmented to twelve. In a short time the fund was over subscribed and the work was carried out later that year. £10 of the remaining money was placed in the Restoration Fund, repaying the grant of ten guineas given towards the bells. Their opening did not meet with everyone's approval and some criticism was expressed at the next Guild Committee Meeting over the way it had been handled. The first peal on the twelve was of Stedman Cinques in 1930, conducted by Tom Hibbert, with many of his College Youth friends in the band. Later that year, the first peal of Maximus rung in Berkshire was scored there, conducted by Frank W. Perrens, with William Pye on the tenor.

The number of peals rung in the twenties was much smaller compared with the pre-war period. From thirty-seven in 1919 it crept up slowly to eighty-five in 1922, and then dropped again to only thirty-nine in the year of the General Strike. For the next three years, it remained at about sixty, rising to ninety-one in 1930.

Although the number of peals was not so high, the quality began to improve. The Locks were active in the North Berks branch, ringing a number of peals of Grandsire Triples in 1921. Subsequently they progressed to Kent, Double Norwich and Stedman and finally they achieved Cambridge Major in 1930.

Before C. A. Valentine's death, the North Bucks branch rang many peals of Minor; his loss was an acute setback to their peal ringing potential. In the Oxford area Walter F. Judge was emerging as a very competent conductor, especially of Stedman. In 1925 he also called the first peal of Little Bob Major for the Guild and the first peal on the new ring of ten at Banbury in 1930. It was most unfortunate that this peal of Grandsire Caters, which included seven local ringers, was later discovered to be false.

The East Berks and South Bucks branch contributed most of the peals in advanced methods. Before the War George Martin had raised the standard of the Boyne Hill band to include peals of Cambridge and Superlative. Afterwards he turned his attention to other members of the branch. A series of practices were held each month at Burnham, restricted to one method only. When everyone had rung a peal in that method, they proceeded to the next. By these means the branch produced some very competent ringers.

London Major was achieved in November 1921; it is interesting to note that the peal board recording it in Burnham belfry was made from a hundred and fifty year-old table top from Burnham Priory. George Martin was not selfish about the conducting and encouraged people like William Welling, Cecil Mayne and George Gilbert to share it. His presence was still in demand though; while he was seriously ill in 1923, not one peal of Surprise Major was rung.

Two long peals were rung at Appleton. The first, on 19th November 1921, was 10,043 Grandsire Caters, composed and conducted by George Holifield, Snr. It took the combined Appleton — Abingdon band six hours six minutes to ring. The other peal was a brilliant effort by four Appleton men, four London College Youths and Tom Hibbert with his son, William. The record states:

APPLETON, Berks.
On Saturday April 22nd 1922, in 12 hours 25 minutes
21,363 STEDMAN CATERS

Challis F. Winney	Treble	Henry R. Newton	6
George Holifield Jnr.	2	Alfred B. Peck	7
William Hibbert	3	Richard T. Hibbert	8
Herbert Langdon	4	Richard White	9
George Holifield Snr.	5	Fred White	Tenor
Composed by Henry G. Miles		Conducted by Herbert Langdon	

This was the longest peal rung by one set of men and only the second occasion the clock had been rung round. It was to remain the record length in the method for over fifty years, and the longest peal in any method up to November 1950.

Other peals of note include one of Grandsire Triples on handbells by George Martin and his family in 1922; this was the first handbell peal for the Guild for eleven years. The first of Stedman Cinques on handbells was rung in London by three College Youths and three Cumberland Youths. Edwin Hims called the first of Bob Minor in hand in 1924 and two years later rang four to a peal of Stedman Doubles — the only time this has been done. He was also the first resident member of the Guild to ring a peal on two tower bells — Bob Minor at Launton in 1926. The first of Bob Major for the Guild in which each member rang two handbells was rung at the "Fleur de Lys" East Hagbourne two years earlier.

The first peal of Spliced for the Guild was of Oxford and Kent Minor at Stoke Poges in 1926, conducted by Arthur D. Barker. George Gilbert called the first of Major three years later at Hughenden. The Vale of the

White Horse branch managed two peals of Grandsire Doubles during 1927. Compared with the achievements of other branches, this may have seemed mundane, but it had involved a tremendous amount of work by a few people. Tom Hibbert and Revd. C. W. O. Jenkyn had spent several weekends at Faringdon, teaching the local band. To use Tom Hibbert's words: "If Alfred the Great could wipe out the Danes at Ashdown, then we could wipe out "stoney" at Faringdon!" These were probably the first examples of one-day courses ever held, and they proved their worth, for after three of them, the local band were able, with help, to ring a quarter peal of Grandsire Triples — a good instance of the dedicated work of the officers of the Guild.

Chapter Eleven

PERSONALITIES

There were many men who enriched the Guild by their skill and ability as ringers. This chapter is devoted to a few of those who were active in this period of the Guild's history.

Canon G. F. Coleridge

Coleridge was born in 1857 at Cadbury, Devon where his father held the living, and he learnt to handle a bell there when he was seventeen. After graduating from Keble College in 1884 he went to Caversham for his first curacy. He was vicar of Crowthorne, Berks from 1904 until his death in 1949.

While he was an undergraduate, his involvement with the Oxford University Society included serving first as its secretary and later as its Master. He was active in the formation of the Guild and later was secretary of the Reading branch for ten years and chairman of the Sonning Deanery branch from 1923-1947.

His first peal was at Kirtlington in 1879 with C. D. P. Davies and F. E. Robinson in the band. His total of 273 peals included many with Robinson, including his 1,000th. He was a fine heavy bell ringer and enjoyed long lengths, taking part in the 15,041 Stedman Caters at Appleton, amongst others.

He was elected to the Central Council when it was established and remained a member until his death, serving as President from 1921-1930. He was a man of strong principles, integrity and humour, and was extremely popular throughout the Guild. His imposing physique and genial disposition made him outstanding wherever he went.

Albert E. Reeves

Born in 1865, Reeves took up ringing when he was nineteen and rang his first peal at Basingstoke; Tom Hibbert and Henry White achieved their first in that peal too. He was a very competent instructor and taught bands at Sonning, Henley, Hurst, Mapledurham and Pangbourne, as well as several others. The Sonning band presented him with a marble clock in 1903 in appreciation of his help. He was Assistant Guild Secretary from

1902, taking over as General Secretary in 1911. He accepted a commission at the start of the War and after a couple of years found that his military duties prevented him from carrying out the secretary's job adequately, so he resigned and R. T. Hibbert took over.

Although he rang a considerable number of peals, he kept no records. He married Mary Chillingworth in 1916 and later retired to her home village, Bradfield, where he died in April 1935.

Richard T. Hibbert

Tom Hibbert was born in the small Berkshire village of East Ilsley on 15th February 1869. He learnt to ring on the five there, but did not progress far until he started as a blacksmith in the G.W.R. workshops in Reading. His first peal was at Basingstoke in 1884, and he soon developed into a fine heavy bell ringer and a good conductor. He was a born leader and a martinet in the belfry. Good peals, rather than lots of peals, were his aim; he used to remark that "good ringing gives me a lump in the throat, bad ringing gives me lumps all over." He constantly sought perfection and woe betide anyone who failed to give of his best. He was nicknamed "The Prince of Strikers."

Although his peal list is not long, it contains many performances of quality. He was the first to ring peals on the heaviest rings of eight, ten and twelve bells: he also rang in the first peal of Maximus at Bow. His long peals included 12,160 Bristol Surprise Major at Knebworth, Herts in 1912, 21,363 Stedman Caters at Appleton in 1922 and 12,675 Stedman Cinques at Southwark Cathedral in 1923. Thirteen years later this magnificent performance was found to be false, and he noted this in his peal book adding "the finest Stedman Cinques I ever heard."

He was instrumental in having the bells at East Ilsley augmented to eight, and the ten at St. Lawrence, Reading made into a twelve. He was secretary to the Guild from 1917-1946. Even so, his heart really was with the College Youths, of whom he was proud to be Master in 1923. A great raconteur, he had a dry humour and could be emotional to a degree, not being ashamed of tears when he was profoundly moved.

He died on 31st March, 1946, aged 77 having rung 375 peals in twenty-four counties.

Joseph J. Parker

Many members of the Guild achieved national ringing fame during their lifetimes. Joseph Parker's ability in the tower was not outstanding, but his name has survived through his gifts as a composer.

He was born at Horton, Bucks on 7th March, 1853 and when he was seventeen he moved to Farnham Royal, where he lived for the rest of his life. He had a shop in the centre of the village and there he plied his trade as a practical boot and shoe maker. He was also the village postmaster.

He was a quiet, genial man who never sought the limelight; he was very fond of a good joke, and had a ready stock of anecdotes. A good musician, he played the violin, the English concertina and gave solo handbell performances. He invented an instrument which played a selection of old shoemaker's rasps by means of a harmonium key-board and he had the honour of demonstrating this to Queen Victoria at an Exhibition.

His first peal was at Ealing in 1883; altogether he rang 131, conducting 56. His last was at Hitchin in 1925, and he had then rung 101 peals of Triples, and the same number of peals for the Guild.

He found lasting fame as a composer. He proposed many new ideas in composition towards the end of the nineteenth century and was a frequent contributor to *The Bell News* and later *The Ringing World*. Many hundreds of his compositions were published, mostly of Grandsire, Stedman and Oxford Bob Triples. He had little interest in Major, but did compose some peals of Treble Bob and Superlative. When his four children were young, they used to help with the proof of some of the peals, writing out leads, etc. Only his elder son became a ringer, amassing a few peals before his death in 1920.

"Old Joe" died on 21st December 1937, aged 84, but his name lives on in his famous Twelve-Part peal of Grandsire Triples, the most frequently rung composition in the method in modern times.

William H. Fussell

William H. Fussell was born on 16th September, 1861 in Upton-cum-Chalvey, a village which is now part of Slough. He learnt to ring when he was fourteen and was encouraged by his brother, who had married the tower captain's daughter. At that time the band was "stoney" and it was several years before he took up change ringing. He worked for a time in architects' offices in Windsor, Reading and London and this brought him in contact with many well-known ringers.

An excellent artist and essayist, he contributed many illustrated articles to *The Bell News* and *The Ringing World*." His first peal was Grandsire Triples at Bicester on 10th April, 1882; he had walked the fifty-three miles to ring it.

He was a good instructor and was employed on a number of occasions by the Hereford Guild. He also worked for the Whitechapel Bell Foundry, which took him all over the country. In the sixty-two years following his first peal, he rang 1,151, of which he conducted 21. These peals were rung in 548 towers, and included one in each county of England and Wales. His 1,000th peal, of Superlative, was rung at Slough in 1934, conducted by George Martin, whom he affectionately called "George III". He was the twelfth person to achieve the landmark of 1,000 peals.

This peal was rung on the eve of his greatest ringing tour — Great Adventure I, the trip to Australia. "Old Bill", as he was known, was an excellent organiser and this excursion for twelve people was a great accomplishment; it captured the imagination of the ringers of England. In 1935, J. S. Goldsmith published a book about it entitled "A Great Adventure".

His last peal was at Slough on 15th April 1944, and he died on 29th August that year, and was buried in Farnham Royal churchyard, not very far from the grave of his former ringing companion J. J. Parker.

Arthur D. Barker

Born on 28th October, 1890 at Islington, Arthur Barker had various jobs — as a motor mechanic, an auctioneer, a hosier and a printer, before he settled down as a clerk with the London Transport Board, where he remained for forty-one years until his retirement in 1955.

He learnt to ring at Islington in 1905 and his first peal was of Grandsire Triples four years later. A good back-ender in his younger days, he has rung a number of "awkward" tenors to peals. He is also a skilful conductor, and was the first person to call a peal of Erin Triples from a non-observation bell. He also called the first ever peal of spliced Oxford and Kent Minor. His longest length is a 7,777 of Stedman Caters at Beddington in 1913. His peal total is about 240.

He has held an office continually in ringing circles for seventy years. From 1911-1924 he was an officer of the London County Association, and from 1924-1954 he was the secretary of the East Berks and South Bucks branch. He was elected Guild Treasurer in 1936, and held this post until 1974. He has been a Vice-President of the Guild since 1961. His other hobbies are stamp collecting and gardening, and he has held Grand Rank in the Order of Freemasons.

In 1922 he married Gladys, daughter of William Bateman, the tower captain at Stoke Poges. She had learnt to ring during the War and rang her first peal at Burnham in 1918. She stood in many early peals for the Ladies Guild, including their firsts of Stedman Triples, Caters and Cambridge Major. She was also the first woman to ring a tower-bell peal of Maximus, in 1921.

Subsequently this talented couple have rung most of their peals together.

Cecil C. Mayne

Cecil Mayne was born at Stewkley, Bucks on 10th August 1892. During the War he opened a cycle business in Beaconsfield, which he later converted to a garage. He left there in 1929, and after a short spell in Bournemouth, moved to Harrow. He travelled the country installing traffic signals and later became station engineer at London Airport prior to its acquisition by the civil authorities.

He learned to ring at Stewkley in 1902 and rang his first peal — Stedman Triples — eight years later at Knebworth. He was a gentle unassuming man, who left his mark on local ringing wherever he went. He was not ambitious in the personal sense, but was always keen to see the band progress. He was an excellent tutor, who had the knack of imparting knowledge, so much so that it appeared that beginners were transformed overnight into safe ringers and good strikers.

In 1926 he was elected the first branch ringing master in the Guild, and with Arthur Barker and others he worked hard in reviving the East Berks and South Bucks branch. He rang 336 peals, of which he called 42; he died from a heart attack on 7th January, 1956.

William Welling

At this period the East Berks. and South Bucks. branch produced many good ringers and conductors, one of whom was William Welling. He came from Long Crendon, where he was born on 18th April, 1885. He moved to Old Windsor when he was eleven and lived the rest of his life there. He was eighteen when he took up ringing and accomplished his first peal at his home tower in 1906, conducted by J. J. Parker. Encouraged by the latter, he progressed rapidly and soon became a competent conductor in most methods.

Bill was a good tutor and started several bands; a number of the ringers he taught graduated to calling peals. He was a link with the older generation of ringers, men like Bert Prewett and Revd. F. E. Robinson, in whose last peal he rang. These men were of the "walking era" when ringers would walk miles for a peal or practice. Bill was of the "cycling era"; he never thought of using public transport, even it if were available, always his bike.

"Old Faithful", as he was known by his vicar, rang 536 peals, conducting 121. He died on 11th January 1962, aged 77.

William Henley

Very few people have been so universally liked as Bill Henley. Born at Sydenham, Kent in 1885, he came to Stoke Poges as a baby of six months. After some elementary schooling, he started work as a blacksmith and was at Stoke Poges Golf Club for nearly all his working life. The magnificent iron gates at the entrance, and all the little individual gates in the Memorial Gardens are his work.

He started ringing at Stoke Poges when he was a lad, and often told the tale that he went up into the belfry each Sunday for two years before they would agree to teach him to ring! His first peal was of Grandsire Doubles in 1901 and during his career he rang over 600 peals in all the standard methods with many well-known ringers. He was as steady as a rock in his ringing: he so rarely went wrong that peals invariably collapsed if he did! He rang at Slough for many years, but when J. J. Parker died, he took over at Farnham Royal and taught a new band.

Although he accomplished so much, Bill Henley was the most modest and retiring of men. He died on 8th July, 1972, aged 87, and his obituary records that: "The Exercise lost one of its most loved, most sincere and most humble of characters, who gained from Heaven not 'a friend' but friends innumerable."

Edwin Hims

Edwin Hims came from Bicester and was taught to ring by Washbrook about 1892. He made very rapid progress and his first peal was one of Stedman Caters at Christ Church in December 1894. He took part in the record peal of London at Drayton in 1896, and the 17,024 Double Norwich at Kidlington. Besides being an excellent heavy bell ringer and conductor, he was a composer of some merit. He composed the longest length of Cambridge Major obtainable at that time — 12,896, which was rung at Stony Stanton, Leics. in 1923.

In 1926 he became the fourth person to ring two tower bells to a peal: 3-4 to Bob Minor at Launton. Later that year he rang 1-2-3-4 to a peal of Stedman Doubles on handbells, a unique feat. Unfortunately he kept no record of his peals.

In the Guild he was active as the secretary of the Bicester branch for eight years, followed by a period as a Guild instructor. He was of a quiet, retiring disposition.

While at work in June 1936, he met with a fatal accident when a crane fell on him.

Richard White

Richard White was born at Besselsleigh, Appleton, in 1878, the son of Frederick and grandson of Alfred White. Like them he followed the trade of bell-hanging, devoting his whole life to bells. A master craftsman, he inherited the business in 1909 and many towns and villages throughout the diocese bear witness to his skill.

His first peal was in 1893 when he covered for Stedman Triples conducted by Revd F. E. Robinson at Great Tew. Altogether he rang about 230 peals, mostly at Appleton, of which over a hundred were on the 9th whilst his brother Fred rang the tenor. Included in his peal records were four long lengths: 10,043 Grandsire Caters in 1921, 16,271 Grandsire Caters in 1932, 21,363 Stedman Caters in 1922 and 12,663 Stedman Cinques in 1944.

. He was a happy man, graced by humility and modesty and full of natural wit and humour. He died on 25th June 1956, aged 78.

Harry Sear

Harry Sear was born in 1878 in Bletchley, two years before his grand-father, Thomas, died. He inherited the family passion for ringing and was taught by his father, Valentine, about 1888. He rang his first peal at Epsom ten years later while he was working in London. In 1899 he returned to Bletchley and took over the teaching of the local band. Two years later he rang his first peal as conductor, in which his father and two brothers also rang.

His marriage in 1908 was performed by Revd. F. E. Robinson with whom he rang several peals. His peals totalled 180, ranging from Doubles to Cinques. He was a founder member of the North Bucks branch and acted as a Guild instructor for many years.

Bletchley valued his services as a ringer, churchwarden, sidesman, and verger, and after his death, aged 86 in December 1964, a stained glass window was erected in the church, commemorating the 111 years' service by his family. The window has two lights, and depicts a bell-chamber with angelic ringers.

Stella Davis

Stella Davis learnt to ring at her home village of Bucklebury, Berks. during the War. After the Armistice, she took a post at a school in Maiden-head, and joined the Guild through the influence of Revd. C. W. O. Jenkyn and Tom Hibbert. A graceful handler and accurate striker, her ability was soon recognised and she was invited into the peal bands operating in the Guild at that time. She kept no record of her peals, but she probably rang between one and two hundred. It is interesting to note that she was the first woman permitted to ring at St. Paul's Cathedral.

She was a faithful Sunday service ringer at Bucklebury all her life, and in 1944, when she was 57, she became tower captain. She was secretary of the Newbury branch from about that time onwards. Her quiet devotion to duty and her popularity led to her election as the first woman Vice-President in 1952.

On 11th June 1960 she was returning home after an outing when she was knocked down and killed in a road accident.

George Gilbert

George was born in Kent on 11th March 1887 and spent his early years at Rainham. His first peal, at Bobbing, Kent, was conducted by W. H. B. Wilkins, another Kent ringer who became a personality in the Guild. George was very fond of Minor, and his first twenty peals were all in seven Minor methods.

An outspoken individualist, he had a generous nature, although he hated "spongers." He was a carpenter by trade, and would often stop by to repair some poor old widow's fence, merely out of charity.

He retired from the Army in 1926 with the rank of company quartermaster sergeant. While he served at Aldershot, he introduced many now well-known people to peal ringing — Charles Denyer, for example. He moved into the Guild in 1928 and joined the tower at Burnham in 1932. He began to build up a peal band and soon became one of the Guild's leading peal ringers.

He was also an eager teacher, cycling miles to help struggling bands. He was somewhat eccentric in the methods he taught; he would not, for instance, teach Surprise methods, claiming them over-rated and only Cambridge "mucked about." In the 1930s he built up a band of young men, but when many of them were called up during the War, he recruited and taught only girls. He was a rigid disciplinarian and he shepherded ninety-one ringers through their first peals.

He was instrumental in getting the old ring of eight at Burnham recast. According to him those bells had a tenor of 16 cwt in K Blunt! He was well pleased with the new light ring of eight cast by Taylors in the 1950s. His peal total was 548, of which he conducted 325, many from the tenor. He died of cancer in Cliveden Hospital on 23rd September 1960, aged 73.

Chapter Twelve

JUBILEE YEAR... AND AFTERWARDS

The Guild was fifty years old on 17th January 1931. The anniversary fell on a Saturday and it is surprising that only two peals were rung that day for the Guild. One was of Double Norwich, conducted by William Welling at Hughenden and the other was an "over-the-border" peal by members of the Gloucester and Bristol Diocesan Association!

The Committee had decided that the event of the year must be the Annual Festival, and for once there was no argument over where it should be held; the Cathedral was the obvious choice. It was planned to offer a free luncheon to everyone who applied for tickets in good time, and the Treasurer was authorised to spend up to fifty pounds. A record number of 340 people sent in for tickets, causing the Treasurer to overspend by nearly £13. Fortunately a donation of this amount from the Master enabled him to keep his books straight!

It must have gladdened the Officers' hearts to see so many people present at the service in Christ Church, which was conducted by the Master, assisted by Canon Coleridge and the Rt. Revd. Shaw, the Archdeacon of Oxford. The preacher was the Bishop of Oxford, Rt. Revd. Strong, who took as his text "I was glad when they said unto me, I will go into the house of the Lord." He expanded this, referring to the part ringers played in the work of the Church, and congratulating the Guild on its long service in the diocese. The collection in aid of the Restoration Fund raised £7 6s, only a few pennies each, a reflection of the shortage of money at that time.

The Chapter House was not large enough so the Annual Meeting took place in the Town Hall. The business proceeded quickly and smoothly and the officers were all re-elected; the only non-routine items considered were some changes to the Rules. One of these, accepted without comment, bound the Guild to the Central Council and undertook that members would abide by its rules and decisions. Another increased the cost of the Report to 4d, a move that many deprecated; they hoped that the price would be reduced in the future.

At the conclusion of the meeting, everyone returned to Christ Church Great Hall, where the luncheon was served. In those times of hardship it was an excellent meal. The first course was salmon, which was followed by a choice of roast beef, lamb, York ham or veal and ham pie, and salads. The dessert consisted of apple tart, fruit salad or wine jellies, and cheese for those who could manage it. There were many guests, including several bishops, the Mayor and Mayoress of Oxford, the President of the Central Council and officers from various diocesan associations. The Report indicates that six "original" members of the Guild attended: Canon Coleridge, J. Jagger, G. Holifield Snr., J. A. Dart, W. H. Fussell and H. Smith.

After lunch the Bishop of Oxford proposed the first toast, "The Oxford Diocesan Guild", to which the Master replied. Canon Coleridge proposed "The Visitors", entertaining the company in his usual witty style, and dwelling on the part played by the Oxford University Society in the establishment of diocesan associations in the South of England. The Mayor of Oxford, Dr. Stobie, gave a short reply on behalf of the non-ringing visitors, and then the President of the Central Council, Edwin H. Lewis, spoke on behalf of the visiting ringers. He had rung with many eminent ringers of the past and he recollected some of his more interesting experiences in their company. Sir George Dashwood concluded the speeches by proposing a vote of thanks to the Cathedral and College authorities, to which Bishop Shaw replied. After the formalities, the ringers dispersed to the towers, but the ringing was not of a very high standard.

The Golden Jubilee was marked in only one other manner: an increase in the number of peals rung. The total of 111 was the highest credited to the Guild since the record year of 1912. About half were rung by members of the East Berks and South Bucks branch; these included 22 of Surprise: mostly Cambridge and Superlative, but several of London and Bristol and one of Cambridge non-conducted. The only other area where peals were scored consistently was around Oxford itself, where Walter Judge's band were proving very competent.

The enthusiasm for peals engendered in Jubilee Year carried on into 1932, when a record of 147 were rung. Firsts for the Guild included Bob Maximus at High Wycombe, and Ashtead Surprise Major at Warfield. Arthur Barker called the first of London Minor and Alan R. Pink the first of New Cambridge Major. In addition local bands rang peals of Doubles at Winslow and Steeple Claydon. Conductors were asked to keep a note of the peals they lost; only two complied but the results were interesting. Stedman was the most difficult to achieve and 21 attempts were lost. The next highest was 15 of Surprise Major. Most failures occurred around the halfway point and the most frequent reason was an error in the method ringing. In only two instances were there mechanical faults; one was a broken clapper and in the other a rope came untucked.

Towards the end of the year the Guild regained the record length of Grandsire Caters. Washbrook's 13,247 at Appleton in 1888 only stood for a year. On 22nd April, 1889, the Gloucester and Bristol men surpassed it at Cheltenham with 15,277. The new record was:

APPLETON, Berks.

On 27th December, 1932 in 9 hours 20 minutes

16,271 GRANDSIRE CATERS

Cuthbert G. White	Treble	R. Thomas Newman	6
William Simmonds	2	F. Donald Boreham	7
Frank Taylor	3	George Holifield Jnr.	8
Richard A. Post	4	Richard White	9
Walter F. Judge	5	Frederick White	Tenor

Composed by G. Holifield Snr. Conducted by G. Holifield Jnr.
The longest length rung in the method.

After 1932 the number of peals rung decreased steadily until it reached a level of only nine in 1941. Even so, much new ground was broken in the thirties. Many Surprise methods, now considered standard, were rung for the first time for the Guild, for example: Yorkshire, Pudsey, Lincolnshire and Painswick. Other methods, some rung for the first time ever, included Windsor, Ipswich, Belgrave, Berkshire, Norfolk, Runnymede, Boveney, Hughenden and Beaconsfield. As you can deduce from some of the names chosen, these were rung by the talented East Berks and South Bucks branch bands under George Martin, William Welling, Harry Wingrove or Alan R. Pink.

Harry Wingrove was born on 12th March, 1893 at Beaconsfield, where he learnt to ring in 1908. He joined the Guild three years later and rang his first peal in 1916, under J. J. Parker. With George Martin as his mentor, he became a competent conductor and his first peal in this role was one of Cambridge in 1929. During the next ten years he called many peals in the standard methods and many in new Surprise methods, supplied to him by his old friend, Gabriel Lindoff. He was a popular member of peal tours, especially Billy Fussell's. His peals totalled about 500, a figure that would probably have reached the thousand mark if he had not been dogged by ill health for the last twenty years of his life.

He was a small man and it was a real joy to see him ringing heavy bells so effortlessly, maintaining a brisk but perfect beat and rhythm. He died on 29th May 1971, aged 78.

The Guild suffered a severe blow in 1933. Early in the year Newbury bells were augmented to ten and on Easter Monday, two weeks after their dedication, an open meeting was held. Ringers came from all over the district and among them was the Master, who drove down from Caversham. He took part in a touch of Grandsire Caters on the new second and declared himself very pleased with the ring. Then he went to listen to them outside the tower; after walking about a hundred yards down the street, he collapsed and died.

All the Guild members were stunned. He had been Master for twenty-four years; his able administration and outstanding ability as a chairman had made him extremely popular. The extent to which he was mourned was demonstrated by the fact that over three hundred people turned up at the little village of East Garston for his funeral. Ringers came from most parts of the country and over a hundred wreaths were sent.

At the Committee Meeting held a few days later Canon Coleridge agreed to carry out the duties of the Master until the Annual General Meeting. At that meeting, he reluctantly accepted the post of Master, declaring that it was a young man's job and not for someone nearer eighty than seventy. He insisted that an assistant was necessary and Revd. C. E. Wigg, an enthusiastic young curate from High Wycombe was elected Deputy Master.

Coleridge was Master for the next thirteen years, but his age prevented him from carrying out his duties as he would have wished. He could not make bell inspections as previous Masters had done and this job devolved to the General Secretary. His parish duties as vicar of

Crowthorne and his bouts of arthritis prevented him from attending all the branch meetings. This work was taken over by the Deputy Master, but the General Secretary continued to try to attend every meeting as well. Coleridge was a remarkable leader; through the force of his personality and his general demeanour he maintained harmony at the Guild's General and Committee Meetings – no mean feat!

The memorial to Jenkyn took the form of a tablet in Christ Church cloisters and the enlargement of the chapel at St. Anne's School, Caversham, where he had been chaplain for over twenty years. A remarkable amount of money was contributed and all the work was completed and paid for before the end of 1934.

Several other well-known men died during the decade. Ralph Biggs, an early member of the Hughenden band, died in 1932 and Frank Hopgood died the same year. He had been a very experienced composer, conductor and peal ringer in the Reading area and had represented the Guild on the Central Council from 1900 to 1932. Edwin Hims, Albert Reeves and Joseph J. Parker have been mentioned earlier. George Holifield Snr. the grand old man from Appleton, died in 1938.

The meetings held during the period were often stormy and controversial. An unsuccessful attempt to unseat Tom Hibbert from the post of General Secretary was made in 1935 when Frederick Sharpe was nominated for the post. The perennial argument over the location for the Festival always came up and the Report was, as usual, a bone of contention. Many were produced but few were sold; sub-committees considered the contents and how to improve them; appeals were made for more people to buy copies. Protests were made at one meeting about the publication in the Guild Report of peals rung for other associations. One year the Report was not issued until June because the Auditors were late in completing their work. This evoked a proposal to elect auditors each year from among the members who would get the audit done on time. After a heated debate, the motion was lost. Some years later, however, the Treasurer was given authority to appoint two auditors if he found that those elected at the Annual Meeting were unable to finish the books before the Report deadline.

In March 1936 a sub-committee was set up to revise the service books, but it did not meet for eighteen months. Two years later the book was ready for publication but the General Committee had a change of heart and shelved the matter. An autumn meeting was suggested in 1937, but was rejected by a large majority.

In 1936 A. J. Wright, Treasurer for thirteen years, retired. He had been in failing health for some time and had found it increasingly difficult to carry out his duties satisfactorily. After he gave up, his health deteriorated still further and he died on 31st October 1939. He was suceeded by Arthur D. Barker, who was also treasurer of the East Berks and South Bucks branch; he was to remain Guild Treasurer until 1974.

The post of Trustee is not arduous but one that demands men of integrity. One such was Leonard J. Joyce, who was appointed in 1933 when Revd. R. W. H. Ackworth moved out of the diocese. Joyce was a churchwarden at St. Mary's Reading and was responsible for the rehanging of the bells there in the '20s. He was an excellent ringer and a popular chairman of the Reading branch. His peal total was not high, probably because of the demands made on his time as a surgeon. He operated on Douglas Bader after his flying accident in December 1931. Joyce continued as a Trustee until his death on 19th March 1939. The other Trustees appointed in those years were Canon Coleridge, and William Evetts of Tackley, Oxon, who was secretary and treasurer of the Witney and Woodstock branch.

Fourteen of the fifteen branches appeared to be managing their affairs well, but membership fluctuated; in general the country branches lost members while those containing large towns tended to gain them. In 1936 the Bradfield branch faced a crisis: three of the eleven towers wanted to join other branches. The impetus for such moves came from the branch secretary, Revd. R. Howes, vicar of Beenham, who had joined the Guild the preceding year and was immediately voted into office. He was a ringing enthusiast and had written an admirable little booklet entitled *Village Bells,* a treatise designed to help self-taught country bands.

Why he thought Beenham and Aldermaston would be better off in the Newbury branch is not clear, but he certainly pressed for their transfer. He may have considered that the standard of change ringing was better in that less rural branch. Burghfield wanted to change to the Reading branch, which made sense for it was on the road between Mortimer and Reading, both already in that branch.

A special meeting was held at Theale to which the Master was invited. As the towers were determined to leave the Bradfield branch, he had no option and reluctantly gave his consent. He strongly disapproved, for it seriously weakened a small branch. In the Report he commented "the strong helping the weak should be the rule throughout the Guild."

In 1934, just three days before his seventy-third birthday, Billy Fussell achieved one of his life's ambitions — to ring a thousand peals. He was the second resident Guild member to reach this landmark; the peal was rung at his home tower, Slough, and some of his old friends took part.

SLOUGH, Bucks.
On 13th September 1934 in 3 hours 10 minutes.
5,088 SUPERLATIVE SURPRISE MAJOR

Leonard Stilwell	Treble	Frank Bennett	5
George R. Pye	2	William Welling	6
George Martin	3	Harry Wingrove	7
William H. Fussell	4	William Henley	Tenor

Composed by N. J. Pitstow. Conducted by George Martin.

Frank Bennett and George Pye had each reached a thousand peals in 1924 and 1927 respectively. Leonard Stilwell, the only surviving member of this band, rang his 1,000th in 1975 when he was eighty-five.

The tourists on the Great Adventure credited three peals to the Guild. The first was of Bob Major, rung on handbells in the middle of the Indian

Ocean. The other two, called by George Martin, were of Kent Treble Bob Major and Stedman Triples — the first in each method to be scored in New South Wales.

The first peal of Spliced Surprise was scored at Whitley Bay in 1924. Touches were rung in the Guild soon afterwards, but the first peal was not rung until 1935 when Alan R. Pink called Cambridge and Superlative at Old Windsor. The year before he had called a peal in three plain methods at Warfield. The first in the four standard methods (London, Bristol, Cambridge and Superlative) was rung at Hughenden by Cecil Mayne's band in 1937.

Other peals of interest included a clerical peal at East Hagbourne in 1935; Revd. C. E. Wigg and Revd. A. G. G. Thurlow, who was then a curate at Wokingham, both took part. The first of Yorkshire Royal was rung at Appleton in 1937 by a touring band, conducted by F. W. Rogers. There was a non-conducted peal of Superlative at Old Windsor in 1938 and the local band rang a peal of Stedman Triples at East Hagbourne in 1939.

After the declaration of War on 3rd September 1939, only five more peals were rung that year. Fifteen were rung in 1940 beore the introduction of the "Control of Noise (Defence) Order" on 13th June. Henceforth bells could be rung only by the military or local defence volunteers. On 16th June a Lincolnshire vicar was prosecuted under the ban for tolling a bell and sentenced to four weeks' imprisonment. When *The Ringing World* pointed out that the Order did not come into effect until 19th June, he was released and his sentence quashed.

The last tower bell peal in the diocese before the ban was one in four Minor methods at Cassington by Alan Pink's band. All tower bell ringing then had to be done on silent bells. At New College, and a few other places, the clappers were removed: generally the clappers were tied when practices were held. Several stratagems were adopted to make the ringing more realistic. The Central Bucks branch had a good idea; each ringer had an assistant who rang a handbell at the right moment in each stroke of the tower bell!

In his report the Deputy Master called for teaching standards to be maintained, and advocated training evacuees so they could help in some of the silent towers in London after the War. The Technical School for the Blind was evacuated to Dorton, Bucks and the Guild organised a course of instruction for them on tower and handbells.

For the first time handbell ringing was seriously practised in the diocese. Old sets of handbells, untouched and neglected for years, were brought out, cleaned and pressed into use. Several bands progressed to the peal ringing stage; the publication of nine peals, as well as the quarter peals rung in 1941, indicate that five separate bands were working hard. Twelve peals were rung in the following year, including two of Spliced Major.

In 1942 the ban was lifted temporarily, first to mark the victory of El Alamein on 15th November and then for Christmas Day. It was lifted altogether in 1943 and our first tower bell peal rung was of Double Norwich at Old Windsor on 3rd July, called by E. C. S. Turner. Of the twenty peals rung that year, ten were on handbells. In 1944 the number of handbell peals dropped to one; there were forty-five tower bell peals. Next year there was one again and eighty-five tower bell peals. Handbell ringing had died out again almost completely.

Two further events of interest took place during the War. The first was the marriage of the Deputy Master. Charles Elliot Wigg was born at Ferry Hinksey in 1908, and after attending Oxford High School, went up to Keble College. While there, he learned to ring and was Treasurer of the University Society in 1930; he rang his first peal in 1931. After completing his training for the ministry at Wycliffe Hall, he took a curacy at High Wycombe. While there he rang numerous peals with Harry Wingrove and Fred Hayes, as well as travelling many miles to assist at practices. He taught many ringers, as well as entire bands at Chearsley and Nether Winchendon.

In 1933 he was appointed Deputy Master and his conscientiousness and devotion to the Guild meant that he spent more time on attending meetings and practices throughout the diocese than on peal ringing. His notebooks testify to the interest he took, not only in the people he met and the bells he rang, but also in the towers themselves and their gear; he was often asked to give advice on restoration work.

In 1941 he married, and the General Committee circulated the branch secretaries, asking if members would like to contribute to a wedding present. Enough was collected to buy a chiming grandfather clock, with an inscribed plate. It was too large to show to people at the Festival so a photograph was handed round! His own branch — for he was then vicar of Chearsley — presented silver candlesticks and cruets.

John Goldsmith the editor of *The Ringing World* had many close associations with the Guild. He could be seen at all the Festivals and frequently rang peals with resident members. In 1942 he became seriously ill and the paper ran into financial problems. An appeal was made to associations for help and the Oxford Guild responded magnificently. The General Committee voted £50 from the Reserve Fund, closing the account, and requested additional funds from the branches. Difficulties arose in some areas, for their Rules did not always permit donations of this kind. Several times the example of the Sonning Deanery was followed; this branch altered the branch Restoration Fund to a Reserve Fund, so that they could send £10. Altogether £120 was sent to *The Ringing World*, sufficient to print it for more than four weeks. Ever since the Guild has made regular gifts each year.

After Goldsmith's death, the production of the paper was taken over by the Central Council, who refunded £10 to the Guild in 1945.

During the 1930s heavy inroads were made in the Restoration Fund and as many as ten grants were paid in one year. By 1939 the fund stood at £102; by the end of the War this had increased to £345, thanks to the skilful manipulations of the Treasurer. The next few years would see many calls upon the fund in the post-war restorations and augmentations.

Chapter Thirteen

REPORTS, RULES AND MONEY!

During the War years the enthusiasm of some of the older members kept the Guild going. Most tower captains know that once a ringer gets out of the habit of attending ringing twice on Sunday, it is very difficult for him to enter into the commitment again. The three year ban on the ringing of bells must have presented a very worrying situation for those dedicated to the preservation of the Exercise. Guild meetings were sometimes depressing; Tom Hibbert recorded in his account of the 1941 meeting "No ringing, no dinner, no tea, but plenty of rain!" It must have been a great relief to the Officers when 174 members attended the 1945 Festival Lunch at Oxford, and many more came later on for the ringing.

The Guild was fortunate in that only sixteen men were killed during the War, a fraction of the 119 who died between 1914 and 1918. Eight branches were spared the loss of any members; the Newbury and the East Berks and South Bucks branches suffered half the losses.

At the meetings that year some books were presented to the Guild by Mr T. Trollope and Capt. A. B. Poyntz, R.N., which formed the basis of the library, and Miss M. R. Cross was appointed Librarian to look after them. The number of books increased quite rapidly as more were presented, and now several hundred books, pamphlets and periodicals make up a fine library for the use of members.

At the next Committee meeting both Canon Coleridge and Tom Hibbert declared that they would not seek re-election. Canon Coleridge was eighty-nine and his doctor had ordered him to do as little walking as possible. Tom Hibbert was not a fit man either and his son, William, had assisted him with the Secretary's work for some time. He died on 31st March, 1946 and the Guild lost one of its most notable personalities. Coleridge said of him "Honest Tom was a prince among men and among ringers."

Fortunately for the Guild, Bill Hibbert was able to pick up the reins straight away and was confirmed in the post of Secretary at the next meeting. The Committee recommended that Revd. C. E. Wigg should succeed Coleridge as Master. At the Annual Meeting, Capt. A. B. Poyntz was also put up; in the subsequent ballot Elliot Wigg was elected by a majority of three votes. The same meeting elected Canon Coleridge a Vice-President, many of those present failing to remember that he had already been elected one — in 1927.

The Report, rules and money seem to have obsessed everyone during the post-War period. Several special sub-committees were set up to ponder these problems, and in most cases their advice was rejected. In 1946 one was appointed to try to improve the Report. Their recommendation was to raise the subscription to 2s 6d to facilitate publishing it. There were also other suggestions about the Annual Festival. When the report was presented, the Secretary was rapped over the knuckles for over-enthusiasm and the report was declared null and void; all the recommendations were ignored.

The sub-committee was re-appointed the next year and then suggested that the subscription should be 3s 0d, which was thought excessive; 2s 6d was the most that people could afford. Even that proposal received only just enough votes — nearly half those present thought the subscription should be 2s 0d! That meeting saw two more decisions made. The Guild recommended that bells should not be rung during Holy Week and the criterion that membership of the Guild also entailed membership of the Church of England was re-affirmed.

Another sub-committee was appointed to raise the £98 15s required to recast the tenor at East Ilsley in memory of Tom Hibbert. By the time the work was completed the price had increased to £121, although that figure included the provision of a brass memorial tablet in the ringing room.

A further example of the lack of money in the Guild was reflected in the affair of the Guild badge, which was discussed originally thirty years previously, but nothing had been done. Thomas J. Fowler revived the idea and it was agreed that one was desirable. He was asked to prepare a design, which he did, producing the master die at his own expense.

The Rules also occupied the members during that time. On at least nine occasions alterations were proposed and finally the situation became so confused that in 1957 another special sub-committee was set up to revise them. Three drafts were made; copies of the second were circulated to every tower for comments before the last draft was settled. At last this received the assent of members at general meeting and was published with the Standing Orders as a sixteen-page booklet in 1958. Everyone hoped that in future only minor revisions would be needed and the Rules in that form would be retained until at least the Guild's Centenary, but it was not to be.

On 22nd November 1949 Canon Coleridge died. His vigorous personality and clear mental faculties remained with him throughout his long life of ninety-two years and he was mourned by many, all over the country. The question of his memorial provoked much argument. Everyone agreed that a tablet should be placed in Christ Church cloisters next to those for Robinson and Jenkyn. The schism was over what else should be done. It was suggested that the two trebles at the Cathedral should be recast as a memorial. More than half of those present at the meeting thought that this idea was too parochial and deferred a decision to the following year. The delay kindled much comment in *The Ringing World* for Coleridge had been a national figure — he was President of the Central Council from 1921 to 1930 — and the rest of the Exercise wanted to see a memorial erected quickly.

In 1950 and 1951 special meetings were held and it was decided eventually to carry out the original plan. The new bells and associated work cost £157, and the two tablets, one in the cloisters and the other in the ringing room, a further £60. It was 1954 before all the work was finished and the account closed.

Discussions on the Report took up an inordinate amount of the members' time. From 1940 to 1947 an abridged Report had been issued, from which the list of members was omitted. In addition there were few peals to be printed. It was decided that a full Report, on pre-War lines, should be issued in 1948. On publication, its cost amounted to two-thirds of the Guild's income for the year. The Report for 1949 was similarly expensive, despite the increased cash flow from the higher subscriptions. The same thing happened in 1950 and the Committee were convinced that printing the 1951 Report in a similar way would bankrupt the Guild. They were able to persuade the members that the production of a double issue for 1951-52 would be better.

Several more special sub-committees were established to find a solution to this problem. The obvious conclusion reached was that more money should be raised and less material should be printed. Neither recommendation satisfied the members. Attempts to charge peal fees were defeated in 1947, 1949 and 1951. A suggestion that future peals should be printed in tabular form was rejected. In 1952 a proposition to raise the subscription to 3s 0d was lost. In 1954 a committee recommended that peals should be deleted and branch reports added. The members decided to keep the peals and have branch reports as well.

Three more efforts were made to alter the subscription. In 1955 a proposal to reduce it to half-price for children at school was lost by only one vote. The next year a further unsuccessful try was made to increase it to 3s 0d, and one to raise it to 5s 0d in 1957 was ruled out of order.

In 1955 a "new-look" Report was produced, which was the work of Philip Walker, a man of great experience in the printing field. Although vastly improved, it was still expensive for it cost £115 out of a total income of £135. Such figures finally convinced the members that they could not afford to print a full Report every year, and from 1956 to 1970 a full was issued every other year, alternating with an abridged version.

During the War the Committee discussed ways of building up the Restoration Fund. In 1942 Capt. A. B. Poyntz suggested circulating all the P.C.C.s in the diocese and asking them to pay 2s 0d a bell to the fund. In the first year this was done; the sum of £30 15s was raised, nearly three times the normal capital income for a year. Subsequently the appeal was repeated, mainly through the generosity of one of the members who paid the expenses. Despite inflation, P.C.C.s managed to remember the 2s 0d a bell: by 1974 the amount collected was still just over £50.

No grants were paid from 1939 to 1949, enabling the Treasurer to accumulate some capital, from which future grants could be met. Most of them were not large, more a token of appreciation than a real financial help. For instance one of the largest was given to Burnham, who received 40 guineas towards their bill of over £2,000 in 1950. Hughenden had similar work done and received £50 two years later. Boyne Hill obtained a similar amount for the restoration of their bells in memory of George Martin who died in 1953.

Several other well-known members died during these years. John Evans, from Hughenden, died in 1946. He had been a very active member from the early days of the Guild, both as an instructor and as a peal conductor. The Guild recognised his valuable work when they elected him a Vice-President in 1933.

James Wilkins died on 4th January 1951 at the age of eighty-eight. He too had been a member almost from the foundation of the Guild, and played an important part in the establishment of change ringing in the area around Boyne Hill. About 1900 he moved to High Wycombe where he continued his work as an instructor.

Victor Bennett was secretary to the Oxford Society for nearly thirty years, and was a well-known ringer in Oxford. He was tower captain at St. Giles and was a popular figure among the many students who passed through the University. Many beginners owed a great deal to his inexhaustible patience. Although he rang less than a hundred peals, his performance did include the record length of Stedman Cinques at Christ Church in 1946 and the first peal of Spliced Surprise in twenty-five methods. It was a sad loss to the area when he died on 23rd September, 1954, aged sixty-two.

Richard White of Appleton died in 1956 as did Ralph Coles, a noted member of the High Wycombe band. In 1957 one of his contemporaries, Fred Hayes died; he had rung at High Wycombe nearly as long as Ralph and was a competent composer and conductor of Stedman on higher numbers.

When Mrs C. W. O. Jenkyn died some four years earlier; she made two important bequests to the Guild. The first was a magnificent model of a bell in its frame, probably made by her husband. This bell weighs about 20 lbs and rests in plain bearings in a frame approximately twenty-four inches by twelve inches. It was decided that the Master should be responsible for it and it has been passed to each successive holder of this office. The second bequest was the sum of £500 which was placed in the Restoration Fund. With the addition of this legacy the fund rapidly built up to the magic four figures in 1956. The balance sheet showed that there was £1,000 2s 2d in the Guilds funds; all but £54 was in the Restoration Fund.

Four new Vice-Presidents were elected for their services to the Guild. Frederick Sharpe, who had established himself as an authority on bells and their gear was elected in 1949. Two years later Stella Davis became the first woman to achieve this honour. Thomas J. Fowler, known as "Uncle John" to nearly everyone, was ringing master of the East Berks and South Bucks branch for twenty-five years. Loved, respected and held in high esteem by all who knew him, he was elected in 1954, an honour well-earned and of which he was justly proud. Thomas Trollope, a senior member of the Guild whom Washbrook had taught to ring, was elected a Vice-President in 1956 when he was ninety-six.

Capt. A. B. Poyntz served as Deputy Master until 1951 when he moved out of the diocese: Frederick Sharpe was a natural successor. There were other changes among the officers. After his father's death William Hibbert continued as General Secretary for ten years. Despite the drawback of living in Hampshire, more than ten miles from the Guild's borders, he travelled widely to branch meetings. His forthright speeches, delivered in the trenchant manner so characteristic of his father, made him known and respected.

On his retirement four members submitted their names for the post. Miss M. R. Cross, the Librarian, was successful in the ballot; the other candidates were Philip Walker, Cyril Kinch and William Butler. The vacant post of Librarian was filled by Mr H. L. Roper.

Changes were occurring in the branches too. The Bradfield deanery had never recovered from the effects of the schism in 1936, and had ceased to be a viable unit by 1951, when it was absorbed by the Reading branch where all the towers happily remain.

The Vale of the White Horse branch continued to operate, even though it had only three more members than the Bradfield branch, and only Shrivenham and Faringdon practised change ringing. Their survival may have been due to the persistence and continuity of service offered by the secretary, R. F. Gilling who had then completed nineteen years in office. He was able to report that out of a branch membership of fifty-six, an average of twenty-four came to the meetings.

The Central Bucks branch also believed in retaining its officers. Canon G. Dixon was their first chairman and he was still in the post twenty-five years later. In 1955 Frank Gibbard was able to report that he had been secretary for a similar period; he was presented with a chiming clock to mark the occasion.

Nine founder members were present at the Golden Jubilee of the North Bucks branch in 1954. The meeting was held at Newton Longville, where the branch had been formed. The membership had dropped considerably in the intervening years: in 1910 they had the second highest membership but by their Jubilee they were seventh.

Newsletters were an innovation in the fifties. The first two to be issued in the Guild came out in 1957. In the East Berks and South Bucks branch their secretary, William Butler, started *The Ringers' Magazine,* which contained a leaflet detailing the activities in the branch. David Smith, secretary of the Witney and Woodstock branch also published one for his area.

In 1956 the Banbury branch suffered a serious blow with the death of Ernest G. Pearson, their secretary for the past twenty-five years. His perseverance had built up the branch; when he died membership was at its highest level ever. Their change ringing capabilities had improved too, for the next year they rang a peal on the rehung eight at Bloxham, the first time a resident branch peal band had been mustered. In the same year the Chipping Norton branch managed a branch peal in the same method at Churchill.

In the realms of peal ringing the Guild was well to the fore. In the immediate post-War years this eminence was due to Walter F. Judge, who was born at Kidlington on 16th November 1895 and learned to ring there when he was ten. He joined the Guild in 1910 and rang his first peal two years later. For a while he worked as a baker at Kidlington and after the War he was employed by Exon, the baker in Dorchester. Eventually he transferred to the confectioners, Oliver and Gurdon, who were just starting up in Oxford and he worked for them for the rest of his life.

After his marriage in 1921 he lived virtually under the tower of New College, Oxford, and soon became well-known throughout the area. He was an accomplished conductor, having an intuitive understanding and an ability to correct mistakes before they took place.

In 1947 he called the first peal for the Guild in the standard eight Surprise methods. The next year he took this up to twelve methods, and by 1951 records were established for the Guild with peals in sixteen, twenty, and twenty-two methods. Finally, the Lincoln Diocesan Guild's record of twenty-two methods was surpassed by a peal in twenty-five methods:

DORCHESTER, Oxfordshire
on 4th February 1951, in 3 hours 20 minutes
5,120 SPLICED SURPRISE MAJOR
in 25 methods, with 149 changes of method

Marie R. Cross	Treble	Richard F. B. Speed		5
Victor J. Bennett	2	Wilfrid F. Moreton		6
Margaret L. Tutt	3	Fredk A. H. Wilkins		7
Alan R. Pink	4	Walter F. Judge	Tenor	
Composed by A. J. Pitman		Conducted by W. F. Judge		

Walter Judge also conducted two long peals: the first was the 16,271 Grandsire Caters at Appleton in 1932 and the other was a new record length of Stedman Cinques.

CHRIST CHURCH, OXFORD
On 24th August 1946, in 8 hours 48 minutes.
12,663 STEDMAN CINQUES

Walter F. Judge	Treble	Fredk A. H. Wilkins		7
Victor J. Bennett	2	Ernest Morris		8
Alfred Ballard	3	Paul K. Williamson		9
Arthur H. Reed	4	Richard A. Post		10
Christopher W. Woolley	5	Richard White		11
Sidney T. Holt	6	Frank C. W. Knight	Tenor	
Composed by C. W. Roberts		Conducted by W. F. Judge		

This surpassed the previous record length of 11,111 rung at St. Martin's, Birmingham, in 1901 by the St. Martin's Guild.

Walter Judge was very critical of poor ringing and always insisted on the best possible striking. He continued to ring and to conduct peals, reaching a total of about 670, before his death on 28th January, 1980 aged eighty-five.

In the 'thirties George Gilbert built up a peal ringing band of young lads at Burnham. The War saw most of them in the Services so he began to teach a band of girls on silent bells. This group achieved a high standard of ringing and in the post-war period scored a considerable number of peals, mostly in Plain and Treble Bob methods.

As the number of peals began to increase, new names appeared. The highest number of peals was 145, rung in Festival of Britain year. New conductors were coming forward too. In 1951 Alan Pink recorded the most, followed closely by William Butler and Robert Blond. Betty Spice, Margaret Tutt and Doreen Coker called peals of Stedman Caters. The latter called the first all-ladies tower bell peal for the Guild at Hughenden in 1956. The Fletcher sisters rang a handbell peal of Grandsire Doubles, probably the first peal to be rung by a band of sisters.

From 1947 onwards more than a hundred peals have been scored each year (apart from 1949 and 1954). In 1954 an analysis of the peals appeared in the Report for the first time for forty years; footnotes were restored in 1955 after a similar time lapse. Alan Pink consistently rang a large number of peals each year, which included many new Surprise methods, Doubles in up to forty-two methods and Minor in up to twenty-two methods. New ground was constantly broken. "Fun" peals included combined Doubles and Minor in 1951 and Oxford and Cambridge Minor on Boat Race Day in 1953. Following the tradition set by Washbrook and Hims, Tony Price from Feltham, Middx, rang two tower bells to a peal of Bob Minor at Tetsworth in 1951; he rang the two heaviest bells, five and six, the first time this had been done.

Other first performances for the Guild were Yorkshire Surprise Maximus at Birmingham Cathedral in 1949, conducted by Walter F. Judge, and silent Plain Bob Royal at Slough in 1955. Two years later seven of this band rang in the first non-conducted peal of Bob Maximus at High Wycombe. New conductors becoming prominent were N. J. Diserens, M. S. Cloke and J. R. Mayne. The latter is Cecil Mayne's son, and although he lives just outside the diocese, and visits it frequently, ringing peals in new Treble Bob and Surprise Minor methods.

Chapter Fourteen

THE WIND OF CHANGE

In the period immediately after the War the majority of people ringing had learnt in the 1930s or even earlier. They had personal contact with the founders of the Guild and had inherited their standards and aims. By 1958 a new generation had been taught whose contacts with the founders were more tenuous. These younger ringers had different standards, ideals and often different goals. They were more ambitious, frequently more highly educated and, in some cases, less tolerant.

Slowly the older men died or retired from active participation in Guild affairs. William J. Paice, a quiet unassuming man and a first class ringer with a wonderful fund of humour and commonsense, died in 1958. He was greatly loved in the Sonning Deanery branch, of which he was secretary from 1927 to 1942. Later that year Walter Sear died; he had been secretary of the North Bucks branch for twenty-five years from the outbreak of the First World War.

Many more of these old stalwarts died in the following years. In 1959 "Uncle John" Fowler and Ambrose Osborne died. The latter was an outstanding figure in Reading ringing circles before the War, always demanding the best a band could give; he had served fifteen years as a branch secretary. In 1960 Thomas Trollope, Stella Davis, George Gilbert, Albert Lock and Edward Foster died. Foster had been elected a Vice-President at the age of eighty only two years before. He had been secretary of the Reading branch from 1932-1946.

Most of these men lived to a ripe old age. Frank V. Sinkins was the son of the Slough workhouse master. The well-known flower, Mrs. Sinkins' Pink, was named after his mother. Frank was the inspiration behind the augmentation of Slough bells to ten in 1951. He died ten years later, aged ninety-six. William H. B. Wilkins, captain of the ringers at St. Ebbe's, Oxford, died the next year, aged ninety-two. He was known to all who rang in the city for his enthusiasm and reliability and did much to encourage peal ringing in the locality. He became a Vice-President four years before his death.

Other notable losses were William Welling, Frederick White (the tenor ringer in the record peals of 1922 and 1932), Harry Sear, the last of the Sear brothers, and Canon Dixon. George Dixon was chairman of the Central Bucks branch from its foundation in 1928 until he retired and moved to Hampshire in 1963. In 1958 he had been elected a Vice-President for his services to ringing in the Guild. He died in 1964, the same year as Kathleen Lock.

Three other deaths ought to be noted. Frederick Selwyn, known as "Feyther" Selwyn in the Banbury branch, had lived and rung there for very many years. After his death in 1968 an engraved clock was placed in Banbury belfry as a memorial. R. J. F. Gilling, J.P., was a farmer who loyally served as branch secretary in the Vale of the White Horse for thirty-four years. He kept this rural area together during a very lean period when no one else was willing to take office.

Capt. A. B. Poyntz died in 1968. He had spent his boyhood at Dorchester, where his father was vicar, before he joined the Navy as a cadet. In his early years he sailed round the Horn under canvas and afterwards he became an engineer officer in the Royal Indian Navy. On his retirement he returned to Dorchester, where he joined the local band, but later he transferred to Goring when he moved there to live. His last home was at Shalford, South Devon. The Guild Library was founded through his initial efforts.

In the realms of peal ringing, bands were growing more ambitious. Peals of Grandsire and Stedman Triples, Plain Bob and Double Norwich Major no longer predominated, except for some of the older, more established peal ringers. Multi-method peals were common and Surprise methods the norm. The first peal of Glasgow Surprise Major was rung at Warfield in 1958, conducted by N. J. Diserens. Two years later the first of Spliced Surprise Maximus was rung at Reading, conducted by W. Williams. Londinium Maximus was called by John Mayne at High Wycombe in 1964, and London Royal a year later at Abingdon. Bristol Royal was rung at Banbury in 1966, called by David P. Hilling, and Bristol Maximus two years later at High Wycombe.

Silent and non-conducted peals continued to be rung in the East Berks and South Bucks branch. Parker's One-Part peal of Grandsire Triples was rung in 1959, seven Minor methods at Hitcham in 1963, Stedman Triples at Stoke Poges in 1965, London Surprise Major at St. Mary's, Reading in 1968 and Yorkshire in 1969. A record was scored for the Guild when a "same name" band rang a peal of Plain Bob Royal:

ST. DUNSTAN, STEPNEY, London
On 10th May 1958, in 3 hours 20 minutes.
5,040 PLAIN BOB ROYAL

William J. Deason	Treble	William A. Theobald	6
William Rogers	2	William C. Porter	7
William Butler	3	William T. Beeson	8
William H. Jackson	4	William Birmingham	9
William T. Cook	5	William Hibbert	Tenor

Composed by William H. Barber. Silent and non-conducted.
The first non-conducted peal rung by a same name band.

The first ever "Michael" peal was also rung for the Guild. This was in 1966 at Great Tew, conducted by Michael Fellows.

Multi-Doubles peals were common; a few years earlier Alan Pink and Elliot Wigg had steadily moved the record up to 42 methods and variations in a peal, which was regarded as extraordinary at the time. The record was taken up to 88, then 105 and finally 113 methods:

HAMBLEDON, Bucks.
On 19th August 1960, in 2 hours 50 minutes.
5,040 SPLICED DOUBLES
Being 42 extents in 113 individual plain course methods, with 350 changes
of method and plain leads used throughout.

Monica M. Blagrove	Treble	William Butler	3
Malcolm S. Cloke	2	Michael Hatchett	4

Frank T. Blagrove   Tenor
Conducted by Frank T. Blagrove.

The greatest number of methods rung in a peal of 5,040 changes.

Six years later a band under Roy H. Jones rang peals in 100, 114, and 126 methods and variations. Another band, under Murray W. Coleman, achieved peals in 77 and 88 methods and variations.

Many more conductors were coming forward, and those consistently calling peals included Howard Oglesby, J. Keith Ward, Edward R. Venn, David P. Hilling, D. Kay Adkins, Frank T. Blagrove, Roy H. Jones, Brian R. White, Robin G. Leale, Christopher J. Rowson, David A. Cornwall, Geoffrey K. Dodd, John R. Mayne, P. G. McIlhone, Frank C. Price and Christopher C. Clarke.

Fig. 26 Joseph J. Parker.

Fig. 27 Edwin Hims.

Fig 28 St. Lawrence, Reading. The first peal in Berkshire was rung here in 1734.

Fig. 29 All Saints, High Wycombe.
The first peal in Buckinghamshire was rung here in 1751.

Fig. 30   Members of the Chipping Norton branch circa. 1908.

Fig. 31 William H. Fussell.

Fig. 32 George Martin.

Fig. 33 East Berks and South Bucks branch, 1932.

Back row: R. Fowler, W. Henley, G. Gilbert, W. H. Fussell, F. Boreham, H. Wingrove, H. Batten, — , F. D. Boreham, — , W. Edwards.

Standing: R. Reid, B. Lister, G. Barkus, A. Bateman, J. Eldridge, G. Martin, J. Taylor, P. Newton, F. West, A. D. Barker, Mrs. A. D. Barker, — , — .

Seated: J. Evans (and grandson), J. L. Kirk, T. J. Fowler, R. T. Hibbert, Revd. C. W. O. Jenkyn, Revd. W. S. Riddlesdell, A. J. Wright, J. J. Parker, W. H. Fletcher, Revd. R. A. Crawley-Boevey.

On ground: W. L. Gutteridge, Mrs. W. L. Gutteridge, Miss F. Gudgin, Mrs. C. C. Mayne, C. C. Mayne.

Fig. 34 St. Mary, Reading.

Fig. 35 St. John, Windsor.

Fig. 36 Vale of White Horse branch 1919.
Standing: R. Wells, T. Dike, — , — , — , F. King, — , W. Edney, — , V.
Goodman, — ,— , — , A. Carter, J. Dowling, C. Carter, W. Wells, C.
Pearce, T. Whiting.
Seated: — , — , Canon G. F. Coleridge, Canon E. F. Hill, Revd. R. J. L.
Newhouse, — .

Fig. 37   Harry Wingrove.

Fig. 38   Alan R. Pink.

Fig. 39 A meeting of the North Berks branch at Harwell in the 1930s.

Fig. 40   Walter F. Judge.

Fig. 41   William Hibbert.
General Secretary
1945-1956.

Fig. 42   General Secretaries.
Kenneth J. Darvill 1976-1981.
Marie R. Cross 1956-1970.
William Butler 1970-1976.

Fig. 43 Central Bucks branch 1958.
From left to right: F. G. Edmans, F. Gregory, L. J. Gregory, Rev. J. F. Amies, Canon C. E. Last, Canon G. Dixon, J. W. Hall, E. F. Gibbard.

Fig 44   St. Michael and All Angels, Hughenden.

Fig. 45   The Guild's Gavel and Stand.

Fig. 46 Frederick Sharpe.
Master 1973-1976.

Fig. 47 William Butler.
Master 1976-

Fig. 48 Members of East Berks and South Bucks branch 1942.

From left to right: A. J. Glass, W. Birmingham, L. Stilwell, W. Welling, W. H. Fussell, G. Martin, A. D. Barker, Mrs A. D. Barker.

Fig. 49 Surprise Maximus handbell band.

From Left to right: D. F. Moore, R. H. Newton, B. F. L. Groves, G. G. Firman, Mrs. G. G. Firman, S. C. Walters.

Fig. 50 Centenary
Festival, July 1981.

The number of new Surprise Major methods rung for the Guild during this eleven years totalled more than a hundred, many of them called by Alan Pink. Seventeen new Surprise Royal methods were rung and twenty-nine Surprise Minor methods, many of which were rung for the first time ever. In 1964 sixty Treble Bob Minor methods were rung spliced together in a peal at West Hanney, conducted by Anthony R. Peake. He also surpassed Walter Judge's peal of twenty-five Surprise Major methods with one in thirty-six methods at Stratton St. Margaret in February 1966. Five of that band rang in a new record for the Guild two months later:

KIRTLINGTON, Oxford
On 23rd April 1966, in 3 hours 8 minutes
5,088 SPLICED SURPRISE MAJOR
In fifty-three methods, ninety-six changes of each, one hundred and fifty-eight changes of method.

Maurice A. New	Treble	Brian Bladon	5
Elisabeth A. G. Bowden	2	Anthony R. Peake	6
Michael J. Hobbs	3	Edward R. Venn	7
John R. Mayne	4	James R. Taylor	Tenor

Composed by W. E. Critchley.   Conducted by J. R. Mayne.

Thirty-nine peals were rung to mark the eightieth anniversary of the Guild and altogether a record number were rung that year. Two personal goals were achieved: Arthur Barker rang his hundredth peal of Stedman and Walter Judge his hundredth peal of Stedman Triples as conductor.

The very select company of men who have rung two tower bells to a peal were joined by two more in 1969. Anthony R. Peake rang the second and third to a peal of Bob Minor at Nettlebed on 25th October and two days later William Butler called Parker's One-Part peal of Grandsire Triples from the third and fourth at Aldermaston. Frank T. Blagrove had already rung a number of double-handed peals for the Middlesex County Association and on 24th June 1961 he conducted for the Guild a peal of Grandsire Triples of his own composition from the treble and second at St. John's, Windsor.

As time passed, peals by entirely local bands became more common, although some were not recorded as such. The first ever by a local band at Ewelme was rung in 1958 — Plain Bob Doubles — and another of Grandsire Triples at Thatcham in 1962. Two other peals of interest were rung that year: one of Doubles on Mr C. O. S. Jarvis' private ring at Balscote Farm, and the first ever peal of Deddington Hybrid Major at Deddington, the first in a "hybrid" principle. The ladies scored a peal of Plain Bob Major at Hughenden in 1966, conducted by Joyce Barton; they were all Sunday service ringers from the East Berks and South Bucks branch.

A new Grandsire Caters record was achieved in 1968, again at Appleton:

APPLETON, Berks
On 10th February 1968, in 9 hours 10 minutes
16,559 GRANDSIRE CATERS

Andrew N. Stubbs	Treble	John H. Napper	6
John W. T. Hibbert	2	Brian R. White	7
Dennis Knox	3	Tudor P. Edwards	8
Frank D. Mack	4	Stephen J. Ivin	9
Dennis A. Leslie	5	Francis A. White	Tenor
Composed by A. M. Tyler		Conducted by B. R. White	

Two years earlier the band at Old Marston, Oxford, had rung a long length of Doubles, which surpassed the record set up 183 years previously at Whaplade, Lincs.

MARSTON, Oxford
On 7th April 1958, in 6 hours 20 minutes
12,600 DOUBLES
in four methods

David C. Woodward	Treble	Malcolm Journeaux	3
Alec Gammon	2	Roy H. Jones	4
	Clive Holloway	Tenor	

Conducted by Clive Holloway
The longest length of Doubles yet rung.

Two other unusually long peals were also rung during the period. In 1967 the highest number of peals — two hundred and twelve — to be rung in a year was achieved and of these, twenty were on handbells. These were almost entirely due to the efforts of Frank C. Price, who rang in eighteen of them. Included were a 7,200 and a 10,080 of Plain Bob Minor, which was the longest peal in hand rung for the Guild.

CROWTHORNE, Berks
On 20th September 1967, in 3 hours 28 minutes
10,080 PLAIN BOB MINOR
14 different extents

Mrs S. O. Sargeant	1-2	Frank C. Price	3-4
	Kenneth R. Davenport 5-6		

Conducted by Frank C. Price
Most changes to a peal by all.

In 1958 a peal of 5,400 changes in sixty Doubles methods was rung on handbells in a Youth Hostel at Inglesham, Wilts, conducted by Brian J. Woodruffe. At that time it was the greatest number of methods rung to a handbell peal. The Guild's first peal of Erin Cinques was rung at Reading in 1964, conducted by J. H. Hunter. Winston Churchill died early in the following year and muffled and half-muffled peals and quarters were rung throughout the diocese. After the interment at Bladon, four Guild and two branch officers rang the following peal:

BLADON, Oxon
On 30th January 1965, in 2 hours 40 minutes
5,040 PLAIN BOB MINOR

Edward D. Patching	Treble	Arthur D. Barker	4
Marie R. Cross	2	Frederick Sharpe	5
David Floyd	3	Canon C. E. Wigg	Tenor

Conducted by Canon C. E. Wigg

As Churchill's funeral train passed through Oxford, Great Tom was raised frame high and tolled by Frederick Sharpe and Elliot Wigg.

A band of enthusiasts rang five peals of Surprise in five different towers in a day, the first time it had been done. They started at Aldermaston on fully muffled bells at 2.50 am, and then went on to Stratfield Mortimer, Thatcham and East Ilsley. The last peal at Highclere finished at 10.07 pm. The methods rung were Yorkshire, Lincolnshire, London, Superlative, and Cambridge and the band included Pat Cannon, George Thoday, Brian Bladon, Geoff Dodd, Philip Mehew, John Hunt and Reg Rex. Most of the band had stood in the three previous attempts when a maximum of four had been rung. Reg Rex took part in all these attempts, ringing with only one arm!

In the 1930s exchanges at meetings were sometimes bitter and acrimonious, although generally only a few people were involved. Despite the size of the General Committee it was possible for the chairman to keep the debates to a reasonable length. Under the Rules operational until 1958, as many as ninety-seven people could have been present at one of these meetings! Considering this figure it is remarkable that the first meeting to continue after tea was in 1950.

The Annual General Meeting was always sandwiched between the Festival Service and the Luncheon. It was held in the Chapter House, notorious for its bad acoustics, and it is certain that many had no idea of the motions they were asked to vote upon. Even so, attempts to transfer some of the business to an autumn meeting met little success until 1957, when the first one was held at High Wycombe.

Procedures at meetings began to conform to modern business practice. Duplicated minutes were introduced by Marie Cross when she became General Secretary and have been used ever since. The new Rules incorporated Standing Orders and occasionally these were enforced. As more keen, young members became interested in the administration of the Guild, discussion sharpened and fewer items were passed "on the nod". Once again money dominated discussions and governed all the decisions made.

In 1956 George Edmans suggested that the Guild and all the branches should each have a banner, similar to those used by the Mothers' Union. This novel ideal created interest, and sparked off the parallel proposal that the Guild should obtain a Master's chain of office and a badge to mark the seventy-fifth anniversary. The sub-committee set up to examine the costs reported predictably that the Guild could not really afford either. A gilt-white metal badge was priced at £31, whilst a silver gilt would cost £36, plus £21 purchase tax. The idea of the badge was shelved.

George Edmans kept alive the interest in a Guild banner and volunteered to have it made for the cost of the materials. It was produced in the village of Great Horwood, Bucks; George Edmans designed it and also turned the cross and ornamental boss from oak taken from the old bell frame. The cloth was woven by another ringer, Mr M. Jamieson, and the embroidery was executed by Miss E. Irving. The Central Bucks branch donated £15, the cost of the materials. The Master, Revd. C. E. Wigg, dedicated the new acquisition in the Cathedral at the 1958 Festival.

Some years earlier another valuable gift was made to the Guild by the Hughenden ringers. This is a gavel in the form of a bell, the stand ressembling a model bell-frame. It was made by Roland Biggs from old oak taken from Hughenden belfry when the new trebles were installed in 1952.

The revision of the Service Book was bandied about by the Committee for many years. Attempts to improve it had been made in the thirties, but nothing came of it for there was no money available for printing. The subject was briefly resurrected in 1949, but it was 1957 before another sub-committee was appointed to re-write it. Like its predecessor, it did not meet for some considerable time, but by the autumn of 1961, it had produced a draft booklet. Twenty-five duplicated copies were sent to each branch and comment invited. There was very little response: the Banbury branch decided by a majority of three to one that they preferred the old book, but that was the view of only sixteen members! The book has remained in draft ever since and most of the present members have never seen a copy.

The seventy-fifth anniversary year, 1956, passed uneventfully. Scattered through the year a few peals were rung to mark it, but only one was rung on the actual day — Grandsire Major at Hungerford by members of the Newbury branch. It was decided that the eightieth anniversary should not go un-noticed, and many peals were rung. On Festival day, a special communion service was held early in the morning at St. Aldate's, Oxford and fifty-three members joined in the celebration of the Eucharist. Later that day the Festival choir performed well. Permission for chorister ringers to robe and form this choir had been given in 1948 by the Cathedral authorities, but it was 1965 before lady choristers were allowed to join.

In November 1961 Elliot Wigg was made an Honorary Canon of Christ Church in recognition of his services to the diocese in the art of ringing. He regarded this as an honour that reflected on the whole membership of the Guild. The Guild honoured the man who had guided their finances for twenty-five years by making Arthur Barker a Vice-President. In 1962 they similarly honoured the retiring Bishop of Buckingham, Rt Revd. Robert Hay, for his service to the Guild.

Reports, once again, occupied a great deal of time. In 1959 the post of Report Editor was created and Philip Walker was the obvious first choice. The sale price of the Reports remained at 2s. 6d., despite the fact that their production cost per copy rose to 5s. 6d. in 1958, 7s. 0d. in 1964 and 10s. 0d.

in 1969! In the even years between 1956 and 1968 an abridged version was issued which merely gave the balance sheet, and reports by general and branch officers. Between 1956 and 1964 Wilfrid G. Wilson arranged for these to be duplicated, and he was elected a Vice-President in 1963 for this and other work.

The subscription remained a controversial issue. In an effort to offset the loss on the Reports, it was raised to 3s. 6d. in 1961, but attempts to put it up to 5s. 0d. or 7s. 6d. in 1965 and 1966 were strongly resisted. In 1969 it had to be raised to 5s. 0d. The accumulated funds reached the £2,000 mark in 1965; £1,766 was in the Restoration Fund, which had been increased in 1961 by another generous legacy of £300 from the Jenkyn family.

Besides the grants given for restoration work each year, one unusual demand was made on the fund in 1968. The church of St.-Peter-in-the-East Oxford, was converted into a library for St. Edmund Hall, and to prevent the sale of the ring of eight bells for scrap, the Guild bought them for £900. They were stored until a suitable home could be found. There were several applications for the Mears' trebles, but only two for the whole ring; these came from Bodicote and Stanford-in-the-Vale. After considering the applications the General Committee eventually decided that the bells should go to Stanford-in-the-Vale, where they were rehung in a new oak frame by Francis A. White. With the money Stanford obtained for selling their old heavy six for scrap, they were able to refund the Guild's expenses and pay for some of the other work as well.

In 1958 the Central Council elected a committee to investigate the state of Sunday Service ringing throughout the Exercise. This Guild had already carried out some research and was able to report that out of 356 rings of bells in the diocese, 27 were unringable. Of the 329 remaining, 75 were silent, 137 were partially manned and only 117 were rung for all the required services. To examine these figures and to suggest remedies the branch secretaries were summoned to a meeting, the first of its kind. Since then they have met annually to consider various problems, mainly in administration.

The survey was widely circulated, going not only to all the towers in the Guild but to the bishops, archdeacons and rural deans, as well as the Diocesan Magazine, which devoted a page to it. The most important outcome of the survey was the knowledge that more and better instruction was essential. The Guild ran a course for potential instructors at Big Wood, Radley over the weekend of 29th April 1960. It was the first weekend course of that type organised by a Guild on its own. It proved very successful and was followed by another at Charney Manor from 5th - 7th November 1965.

The branches tackled their training in their own way. The East Berks and South Bucks, Central Bucks, South Oxon, and Witney and Woodstock branches ran one-day and half-day courses. The North Berks instituted a policy of a strong tower adopting and helping a weak one. The Banbury branch opted for more social events to develop increased awareness among members. The Sonning Deanery organised some training afternoons. Most of the others seemed to have ignored the survey, although the

Newbury branch did discuss it. They were not in favour of Guild organised ringing courses, and did not consider it worthwhile to run one themselves.

The Chiltern branch ran several courses during the 1960s. It had come into existence as a result of a branch secretaries' meeting when they were asked to look at branch boundaries. They recommended the formation of a new one, centred on Aylesbury and taking in remote towers in the South Oxon, Central Bucks and East Berks and South Bucks branches. Donald Wheeler, who had been secretary of the Central Bucks branch, became the first secretary of the new Chiltern branch when it came into being in January 1962.

The branch started well, electing fifty-one new members in its first year out of a total of sixty-eight. The membership did drop in succeeding years but has since stabilised around the sixty mark. The Vale of the White Horse went through a bad time prior to the death of R. F. Gilling when the numbers dropped to only sixteen. Later, it too revived. For the first time since before the War the Chipping Norton branch's membership reached a hundred in 1962. Two years later Jack Keyte, their branch secretary, retired after forty-three years in office.

New people came forward to participate in Guild affairs. Mr H. L. Roper retired as Librarian in 1964 and was made a Vice-President for his past services. His place was taken by Revd. Eric Wood, vicar of Mapledurham and later of Drayton. Oswald Francis, the auditor, retired in 1961, having performed that task for very many years; he too was made a Vice-President.

In 1966 the wind of change stormed through the Guild. The idea of dividing the diocese was seriously discussed by the senior diocesan officials, and the effect of such a move on the Guild perturbed many members. Each branch was asked to comment on two suggestions. The first asked if the branches would like to become autonomous, sending a representative to a Diocesan Council of Ringers. The second was that the Guild should remain as it was, save that the size of the Committee be reduced and that government be vested in it. Whatever choice was made, some changes would follow. There had been agitation at Committee meetings for an amendment to the Rules so that considered judgements could not be set aside by hasty, ill-formed decisions at general meetings.

The branches reported that they were in favour of the second idea. The smaller units knew that they could not survive on their own; the larger ones thought that fragmenting the Guild would weaken it too much. The talks on the division of the diocese came to nothing and the matter was dropped. Even so, it was decided to implement the suggestion of vesting the government of the Guild in the Committee.

Various anomalies had arisen in the 1958 Rules so a complete revision was undertaken. Kenneth Leach, of Wantage, prepared the first draft and several extraordinary committee meetings were held in 1968 to discuss it. The final version was passed at an extraordinary general meeting of the Guild in 1970, which only sixty-six members bothered to attend. The session lasted three hours.

Frederick Sharpe had queried his re-election as Deputy Master in 1965, as he felt a younger man should take on the post, and in any case his work on bell inspections did not allow time for him to visit branches and attend their meetings. The meeting did re-elect him and also appointed Stewards, whose job was to represent the Master and Deputy Master at branch meetings. The first three men in these posts were John C. Baldwin, Walter Hunt and Howard Oglesby. They were elected in 1966 but two years later Walter Hunt left the diocese. No replacement was found for him until 1970.

Ringing matches were thought to be an abomination by the Victorians; in 1864 one writer commented that it was as bad as having a prize fight in the belfry on Sunday! By the 1960s this very narrow-minded attitude had nearly disappeared, and striking contests were held again. Probably the first in the Guild was held in 1960 in the Sonning Deanery, and the Witney and Woodstock branch held one the following year. A six-bell inter-branch contest was suggested in 1963 and the first was held at Radley in '64. The judges were Wilfrid G. Wilson and Richard F. B. Speed, who placed Hughenden first, with East Ilsley, Eynsham and East Hagbourne runners up. It was such a great success that it was determined to hold one every year, and during this period, Warborough, Thatcham, and St. Mary's Reading were the winning teams. In 1969 Edward J. Peett presented a silver cup which is awarded to the winners each year at the Festival. Ernest E. Gosling has prepared illuminated certificates for each of the first three teams since the contest started, and also writes the results in a bound book kept in the Library.

The sixties concluded with more innovations. The Chipping Norton branch held a Ringing Festival, fourteen towers were opened and over a hundred people joined in and took part. The Witney and Woodstock branch sent a questionnaire to all their towers for comments on Guild and branch activities. The results indicated that more social events were required and more support given to ringing meetings. Lastly, the South Oxon branch held a quarter-peal month to mark the end of the decade. A quarter was rung in every tower in the branch and fifty-four of the eighty-four members took part.

Chapter Fifteen

APPROACHING THE CENTENARY

In 1969 Marie Cross gave notice that she did not wish to stand for the post of General Secretary again. There had been only four holders of this office in the preceding seventy-five years and none of them had seen the variety of changes which took place during the fourteen years she had served. Lots of functions, now taken for granted, were her innovations — the autumn meeting, the secretaries' meeting, the Striking Contest, ringing courses, and many more. On her retirement the master presented her with a cheque for £125, subscribed by members from all over the diocese.

William Butler and John Rance competed for the job, and the latter was defeated in the ballot. At the same meeting Marie Cross was elected a Steward, filling one of the vacancies. Mrs A. D. Barker became a Vice-President and in 1971 Miss Cross and the retiring Bishop of Dorchester, Rt. Revd. D. G. Loveday, were also elected. Other men who have served as Stewards in the years up to the Centenary are David A. Cornwall, Timothy G. Pett, Donald G. Wheeler, Barry J. Davis, Peter G. Davies, Henry Lawrenson, Peter J. Heritage, Andrew Haseldine, Graham J. Clifton, Howard W. Egglestone and Noel J. Diserens.

Canon C. E. Wigg moved from Wavendon, Bucks, on the Bedfordshire border, to Hook Norton, Oxon, in 1968. During his ministry there he was never entirely fit, but in 1971 he was very pleased to conduct the marriage ceremony of the new General Secretary and Jennifer Barker at Thatcham. Fifty-five years before, Jenkyn had performed a similar solemnisation for Reeves when he was General Secretary.

In 1972 Elliot Wigg suffered a stroke which partly incapacitated him and he announced that he intended to resign from the Mastership. At the Annual General Meeting at Bicester in 1973, he left the Chair for the last time, after forty years in office; thirteen of those as Deputy Master and twenty-seven as Master. A collection had been made for him all over the diocese and he was presented with a cheque for £215 by the new Master, Frederick Sharpe.

Frederick Sharpe was born in Launton, Oxon, in 1905 and he lived there all his life. When he was fourteen he started ringing and became tower captain eight years later, a post he held until he died. In 1922 he rang his first peal, one of Bob Minor; altogether he rang about forty. He was not such an accomplished peal ringer as his predecessors, but he had a great deal to offer the Guild in other ways. He was able to ring two tower bells to touches and even to quarters, but never aspired to a double-handed peal. He was secretary of the Bicester branch from 1928-1948.

He was churchwarden at Launton for forty-four years, and gave generously of his time and talents in the parish. As a licensed lay reader he was in constant demand to help out in the Bicester deanery. His interests ranged over topography, architecture, railways and, of course, bells. His enthusiasm was fostered by H. B. Walters, whom he helped with bell inspections when Walters became less agile at the end of his life.

Fred Sharpe's books on the county histories of bells began with *Church Bells of the Deanery of Bicester,* published in 1932. His other works include *Church Bells of Berkshire, Oxfordshire, Radnorshire, Cardiganshire* and *The Channel Islands. Herefordshire,* the last part of which was published in 1975, is a monumental work, profusely illustrated with the author's own photographs, and it contains a wealth of information.

He was the owner of a building firm, Lewis Penn and Co., who specialised in quality building work. The bell inspections he carried out, the meticulous records he kept, and the advice he gave demonstrated his professional approach. When Edwin H. Lewis retired as President of the Central Council, Fred was elected his successor and held the post for two terms, from 1957 to 1963. He also served as librarian for many years. He was elected a Vice-President of the Guild in 1949 and Deputy Master in 1951.

The new Deputy Master was Timothy G. Pett, who had served as a Steward for the previous two years. It was not long before there were other changes among the General Officers. Having served as librarian for ten years, Revd. Eric Wood wished to retire. His resignation took effect at the 1974 Annual General Meeting at Kingham, and Philip Walker took his place. The members were very surprised when Arthur Barker refused the nomination for Treasurer. He had faithfully carried out the task for thirty-eight years and most people had never known anyone else in the post. He was presented with a cheque at the following meeting in thanks for all his past work.

Howard Oglesby was elected the new General Treasurer and Ronald A. Thorne the new Report Editor, and they continued in office for the next two years. On 7th March 1976 everyone was shocked by the news that Frederick Sharpe had died peacefully in his sleep. He had suffered a severe heart attack in 1968, but he recovered and resumed his usual hectic life until the end. The Guild had barely recovered from this news, when it was announced that Elliot Wigg, his predecessor and old school friend, had also died. He had left Hook Norton in 1973 to take a less arduous living at Launcells, Cornwall, but his health continued to deteriorate, and he was forced to give up the ministry he loved. He returned to live just outside the diocese, at Moreton-in-Marsh, where he died in hospital on 8th March, 1976.

. Memorial services were held in Christ Church Cathedral. Frederick Sharpe's was on 20th March and the Central Council Administrative Committee arranged to have its six-monthly meeting in Oxford that day, so that its members could attend. More than two hundred people were present from Guilds and Associations all over the country. The service for Elliot Wigg was held on 3rd April, and nearly as many came to that: these were mainly Guild members. The Dean of Gloucester, Very Revd. A. G. G. Thurlow, who had known both men extremely well for many years, gave the address on each occasion.

A joint memorial fund was established by the General Committee, a move which met with some criticism because the two men had not achieved equal prominence nationally. Ultimately nearly £800 was raised and memorial tablets were placed in the cloisters at the Cathedral, joining the others commemorating the Guild's previous Masters. They were dedicated at a moving service at the 1978 Festival in which the Launton Handbell Ringers, originally formed and led by Frederick Sharpe, took part. The bulk of the money raised was added to Nether Winchendon Bell Restoration Fund; both men had had close associations with that tower.

Shortly after Frederick Sharpe's death the General Committee decided that the Deputy Master, Timothy G. Pett, should act as Master until the Annual General Meeting in the autumn. At that meeting William Butler was elected Master, relinquishing the post of General Secretary which he had held for six years. Timothy Pett was re-elected Deputy Master and Kenneth J. Darvill, a past secretary of the East Berks and South Bucks branch, was elected General Secretary. Henry Lawrenson filled the vacant Trusteeship.

There were more changes in 1979, when Mark E. Dobson became Deputy Master and Brian J. Gatward took over the job of General Treasurer. Christopher Parkinson replaced Ronald Thorne as Report Editor and Timothy Pett undertook the post of Peal Secretary, which was created in 1976 and till then carried out by Peter G. Davies. Two new Vice-Presidents were elected: Francis A. White, the Appleton bell-hanger, in 1978 and Philip Walker, librarian and former Report Editor, in 1980.

Many other links with the past were severed during the decade. In 1970 Cyril J. Hibbert of East Ilsley died; he was a nephew of Tom Hibbert and was well-known for his meticulous striking in the true Hibbert tradition. Harry Wingrove, of Beaconsfield, died the following year. William Henley, another much loved member of the East Berks and South Bucks branch and a Guild member for sixty-six years, died in 1972. William Collett of Oxford, who died the same year, was a member for nearly as long and had held office in the City branch for forty-six years, first as secretary, then chairman and finally as a Vice-President. Adrian D. Tyler from Long Crendon was tragically killed in a road accident, and the Guild was deprived of a young man whose ringing future looked very bright. Two members of the Sonning Deanery branch died in 1979; Bernard Castle, branch secretary for twenty-eight years until he retired in 1971 to make way for a younger man, and Vera Robinson, the last surviving daughter of Revd. F. E. Robinson.

In these ten years the word "communication" was used a great deal. Members wanted information and several branches discovered that one of the best ways to disseminate it was by newsletter. The two begun in the fifties had not stood the test of time. 1970 saw the first issues of the one produced by the South Oxon branch. The Banbury and North Berks branches followed suit in 1971, and Newbury started one in 1972. The Witney and Woodstock branch was the last to begin one which is still in existence today; theirs dates from 1973. Several other branches have produced short-lived newsheets, but the difficulty of finding editors has made them ephemeral. A Guild newsletter failed for the same reason.

The economic situation and inflation were reflected by the Guild subscription, which was increased five times during the 1970s. From 1969 to 1972 it remained at 5s. 0d. Decimalisation seemed to put up costs all round, and the subscription did not escape, going to 35p in 1972. From there it went to 50p in 1974, 60p in 1976, 70p in 1978 and £1 in 1980.

The 1970 General Committee pondered for a long time about giving grants for augmentations. The revised Rules did not allow for them, although money had been given for that purpose as long ago as 1895. Faced with the alternatives of creating a new fund for augmentations only, or changing the terms of reference of the Restoration Fund, they eventually opted for the simplicity of the latter.

The new Rules came into force in January 1971 and many members had failed to realise their full effect. Government of the Guild had passed from the members at Annual General Meeting into the hands of the

Committee, whose decisions could not be amended at the Annual General Meeting. There was some contention at the meeting at Dorchester that year, but subsequent meetings have proved to be shorter and less argumentative.

In 1971 at the instigation of the General Secretary, the Central Council decided to carry out another survey on Sunday Service ringing throughout the country. The pilot survey was carried out in this diocese; seventy per cent of the forms were completed and returned. After comparison with the 1958 Survey, it was apparent that the number of towers where the bells were unringable had increased very slightly; even so it was only half the national average. More towers were fully manned, with more women and children coming forward as recruits. The length of time the bells were rung for service was reduced and many more towers rang for one service only instead of two.

Bands reported the lack of enthusiastic leaders, and nearly half said that they needed help. Towers with good service bands credited their success to the ringers attending church; weak towers generally blamed their state on the migration of ringers. Migration has always been a problem in country towers; one incumbent wrote, explaining he had no ringers because "we are a village of ninety, mostly nearing that age!"

Copies of the eight-page report on the results of the survey were widely distributed again. After considering it the General Committee formed an Education Committee to co-ordinate training throughout the diocese. Since 1972 this Committee had met frequently and worked hard to raise the standard of ringing, improve teaching methods, encourage recruiting and educate the general public.

One of the Education Committee's first tasks was the organisation of another residential weekend course for potential leaders. Easthampstead Park, a magnificent country mansion now used as an adult education centre, was the chosen venue and the first course took place in September 1973. It proved very successful and has become an annual event — provisional bookings have been made till the middle 1980s. Several people who attended the initial courses have since served as branch officers.

Great emphasis has been placed on one-day and half-day courses, which are now run in nearly all the branches. Time and time again it has been demonstrated that a learner will benefit more from a single one-day course than from several branch practices. A special feature has been a maintenance course, aimed at steeplekeepers and covering theoretical and practical aspects. Preventative measures taken at the right time can save P.C.C.s thousands of pounds.

The Education Committee failed in one project. They tried to re-introduce the idea of Guild Instructors, who would help silent towers start up again. The Guild had made rapid progress because of the Instructors' work in the 1880s. Little advantage had been taken of them in the 1930s and they were not appointed after the War. The General Committee decided that sufficient voluntary help could and would be found if requests were made through the General Secretary, and the matter was dropped.

The public knows little about the Exercise and many ringers know little other than the practical side of the Art. In conjunction with the Workers' Educational Association or the Local Education Authority, evening classes were organised, courses generally lasting for ten weeks. Subjects included the history and use of bells, their founding, tuning, hanging and ringing, bell archaeology, ringing history, maintenance; rope-splicing and other practical matters were covered. Tune ringing and change ringing on handbells proved popular. The first such course was held in Newbury in 1973 and attracted a record crowd of fifty-seven students, a mixture of ringers and laymen! Subsequent courses were not so well attended, but have been held at Reading, Abingdon, Langley, Tilehurst, and Chinnor.

*   *   *   *   *   *

The Striking Contest continued to grow in popularity, and the East Berks and South Bucks branch showed its strength, winning seven out of eleven contests. The winning bands were Hughenden (three times), Amersham (three times), High Wycombe, St. Mary's, Reading (twice), Wantage, and Easthampstead. In the Centenary Contest at Cheddington, Bucks, Caversham were the victors by a narrow margin from Thatcham.

The first eight-bell contest was held in the East Berks and South Bucks branch in 1966 and another was held in the Sonning Deanery branch five years later. After an abortive attempt to start a Guild-wide competition in the mid-seventies, one was arranged as part of the Centenary celebrations. Branch teams and individual tower teams were invited to take part and in the final at Harwell, the Newbury branch was awarded first place and was presented with a shield given by the Master.

Branches have acquired their own trophies for their own contests. The Lorna Newton Cup is awarded at a competition between the unsuccessful teams in the East Berks and South Bucks branch contest. The winners and runners up are barred from entering for two years, thus encouraging less able teams to take part. The Orchard Cup is awarded to the winners of an annual battle between the Central Bucks and Chiltern branches. It was given to foster greater co-operation and friendship between them. The Clifford East Shield is given to the winning team in the Bicester branch competition and Malcolm Hooton has presented a handsome trophy for the winners in the North Bucks contest.

The Tewkesbury Shield is an inter-association striking contest which first took place at Tewkesbury in 1973. Initially it was for the three local associations, but in 1975 the Guild was invited to enter a band. The test piece was Erin Triples and the Guild was placed first, with the Gloucester and Bristol Diocesan Association in second place. We were invited to return in 1976 when the test piece was a touch of Grandsire Caters and our success of the previous year was repeated. In 1977 the method was Little Bob Royal, but we were fourth behind the Stafford Archdeaconry Society, the Gloucester and Bristol, and the Worcestershire Associations. Since then we haven't been asked to participate!

*   *   *   *   *   *

The change in county boundaries brought about by the Local Government Act 1972 affected many towers on the Oxon/Berks border.

These changes caused the North Berks branch some embarrassment, for they found that all their towers were suddenly in Oxfordshire! A ballot was taken among the members to select a new name and eventually the Old North Berks branch was chosen. At the same time the Banbury branch considered changing its name to North Oxon, but the proposal was defeated by a comfortable majority. Sixteen years before the Bicester Deanery branch had discovered that some of their towers were not in the deanery and they changed the name to Bicester and District. For all this time Cyril Kinch was their secretary; he had served for twenty-seven years when he retired in 1975.

Branch outings became more popular and the Witney and Woodstock ran two unusual events. The first was "Steam and Stedman" in 1971 incorporating the organiser's love of trains and ringing. The second was an outing by launch in 1974. Several branches marked anniversaries by special ringing and social functions. The Central Bucks celebrated their Golden Jubilee in 1978 and the Old North Berks their Diamond Jubilee in 1980. The East Berks and South Bucks achieved their centenary in 1979 and the Sonning Deanery theirs in 1980.

Interest in the Annual Festival waned during the seventies and attendances dropped. It had always been held in July until 1969, when it was transferred to an October date at the request of the College authorities. In 1976 they decided that the only month available for the Guild to use the Dining Hall was January, so the 1976 Festival was held in January 1977! Few people came and the Committee decided that the Festival must revert to July, and a meal should be arranged elsewhere in Oxford. After the dedication of the memorial tablets in 1978, the luncheon was held in the Clarendon Press Institute; unfortunately this was also felt to be unsatisfactory. An informal buffet lunch was tried the next year, and the lowest ever attendance was recorded. Only a Service was held in 1980.

It was decided to make the Centenary Festival as memorable as possible, and the College authorities consented to the Luncheon being held in Christ Church Dining Hall in July. It was preceded by an impressive service, at which the Dean of Gloucester gave the address. The singing was led by an excellent choir of about three dozen ringing choristers gathered from all over the diocese. After the group photograph had been taken, about a hundred members and friends sat down to a five course meal, and heard speeches by Marie Cross, the Very Revd. E. W. Heaton, Dean of Christ Church, and the Master.

In 1977 a sub-committee was set up to plan the events for the Centenary. Amongst the tangible souvenirs produced were bells, goblets and rose bowls in Caithness glass; pint and half-pint pottery mugs, ties, and a new Guild badge. This small, blue enamelled badge has replaced the larger chromium plated one, the die of which had worn out.

The sub-committee recommended that a Master's badge be obtained to mark the Centenary. Guild members were asked to submit designs, and from about a dozen, Stanley G. Scott's was selected. After some minor modifications it was produced in sterling silver at a cost of £372. Donations of £131 were sent in by individuals and some of the branches.

The badge was dedicated at the Centenary Service on 17th January 1981 at St. Mary's, Reading by the Bishop of Reading, who also gave the address. Later that evening several hundred people attended a social gathering in the Civic Centre, where they were able to chat and meet old friends, as well as enjoying entertainment provided by the Aston Clinton Folk Group, the Launton Handbell Ringers, and six Guild members who rang a sparkling touch of Bristol Surprise Maximus.

*   *   *   *   *   *

At the beginning of the decade there were still considerable arguments over the new rules. A whole series of amendments were proposed and discussed at three Committee meetings. At the following meeting in 1973 all their work was wasted, for the changes were all rejected. Some people were so incensed that a motion was passed forbidding any alterations to the Rules for three years, unless they were vital to the well-being of the Guild. Since then the only change has been to make the Restoration Fund into a charity. The 1980 meeting recommended that when these formalities have been completed, the Rules should be printed and circulated.

Three Report Committees met, in 1969, 1975 and 1976. The first recommended that for a two year period members' names should be omitted and that peals should have a one-line entry, including *The Ringing World* reference, and this was done from 1971. In 1974 the members' names appeared again, but it was 1978 before the peals were published in full.

One of the reasons for these changes was, of course, lack of money. Raising the subscription by ten pence a year invoked countless recriminations, despite an inflation rate in double figures for most of the period. Two long standing bones of contention were removed in 1977: the subscription for hononary members was abolished and peal fees were introduced. Finally it was agreed that these were necessary and a charge of 10p per person per peal began on 1st January 1978.

Handbell peals became an important factor in the peal totals. In 1970 seventy-one were rung out of a total of a hundred and eighty-two; for the remainder of the decade they averaged about fifty a year. A significant amount were on higher numbers or in advanced methods. An influx of experienced ringers accounted for this progress. Bernard F. L. Groves came from the Cheshire band to Reading; Christopher J. Rowson, who had learnt to ring at Abingdon and gained most of his handbell experience at Birmingham University, moved to Maidenhead; N. David Lane arrived from the Wirral and David F. Moore from Leicester. Frank C. Price, Kenneth R. Davenport and Noel J. Diserens already lived in the south-east corner of Berkshire, and with Jennifer A. Dunning and Keith J. Walpole (who travelled down from London) many new methods were rung up to and including Kent Treble Bob Fourteen and Cambridge Maximus. With Robert H. Newton three of these ringers rang the standard eight Surprise Major methods, and followed this later with eight-spliced.

During the early seventies further firsts for the Guild were added: London and Bristol Royal, Yorkshire and York Maximus and the first handbell peals ever of Swindon and Littleport Little Royal, Newgate and Bristol Maximus. Peals of Bristol Maximus on tower bells were a rarity then; ringing one in hand was an extraordinary feat.

Several of the ringers left the diocese and a new band was built up. From September '74 until February '75, they rang peals in the "standard eight" Surprise Maximus methods — some for the first time ever — Spliced in ten methods, and in April they accomplished a record peal of Cambridge Maximus:

LANGLEY, Bucks
On 9th April 1975, in 5 hours 50 minutes
10,560 CAMBRIDGE SURPRISE MAXIMUS

S. Clarke Walters	1-2	Graham G. Firman	7-8
David F. Moore	3-4	Katharine J. Maundrell	9-10
Bernard F. L. Groves	5-6	Robert H. Newton	11-12
Composed by R. W. Pipe		Conducted by D. F. Moore	

Umpires: F. T. Blagrove, N. D. Lane and D. C. Brown

The longest length of Surprise to be rung on handbells.

David Moore's work took him abroad for a year and the rest of the band rang peals in the standard Surprise Royal methods and four spliced "all the work"; these were all firsts for the Guild. On 26th May 1976 they were joined by David C. Brown and Paul N. Mounsey for the first peal ever of Cambridge Fourteen and a month later an "all resident" peal of Kent Sixteen was rung.

In 1977-78 the band which had rung the record length of Cambridge went on to complete the Surprise Maximus alphabet, including peals of Strathclyde and Belfast, two very difficult methods. In addition they rang peals of Bristol Major, Royal and Maximus in a day in 1978.

Clarke Walters left the area and his place was taken by Edward J. Futcher in a peal of thirty-five spliced Surprise Maximus on 6th March 1979; this contained the most methods rung to a peal of Maximus on handbells. An even more spectacular peal was rung in the next year. David C. Brown replaced Eddie Futcher and 110 methods were rung — not once, but three times! This is the highest number of methods which can be rung in a normal length peal and comprise one lead of each method.

SLOUGH, Berks
On 7th January 1980, in 2 hours 58 minutes
5,280 SPLICED SURPRISE MAXIMUS
In 110 methods, 48 changes of each

David F. Moore	1-2	Graham G. Firman	7-8
David C. Brown	3-4	Katharine J. Firman	9-10
Bernard F. L. Groves	5-6	Robert H. Newton	11-12

Composed by N. Bennett and J. H. Fielden, Conducted by B. F. L. Groves

The most Surprise methods yet rung on handbells.

At Amersham a band composed of Jean A. Darmon, Stanley E. Darmon, Kenneth J. Darvill and Robert H. Newton have been working through the "standard eight" Surprise Major methods and have gone on to ringing peals in up to twenty-spliced. With the addition of Angela M. Darvill they have rung peals of Surprise Royal. In 1980 other bands have taken up handbell ringing, and peals have been rung at Wokingham, Reading and Thatcham.

In the tower some equally brilliant performances have been achieved. The '50s and '60s saw an increase in the numbers of peals in new methods but the extension of methods to the higher numbers of bells and the growth of multi-method and spliced ringing have characterised the '70s. Belfast Maximus was rung at High Wycombe in 1970, conducted by John R. Mayne. The first for the Guild of twenty-three methods "all the work" Surprise Major was rung at Dorchester the same year, conducted by Timothy G. Pett. He also called a peal at Newbury in 1975 of Surprise Royal in fourteen methods, each lead of which was different.

In 1971 Timothy Pett's band attempted to ring the maximum number of Surprise Minor methods in a peal. They worked their way up through 30, 90, 100, 125, 206 and finally 210 methods or one lead of every method in the peal:

HINTON WALDRIST, Berks
On 24th January 1972, in 2 hours 32 minutes
5,040 SPLICED SURPRISE MINOR
210 methods in seven extents

Richard W. Butler	Treble	Timothy G. Pett	4
Anita D. O'Brien	2	William Butler	5
Brian Bladon	3	Anthony R. Peake	Tenor

Conducted by T. G. Pett ~

Six weeks earlier they had rung a peal of 230 methods in eight extents at Castle Eaton, Wilts, which was the greatest number of methods rung to any peal at that time.

Five members of the band took part in a peal of Caters a year later which contained 100 methods, the greatest number of Caters methods to be rung to a peal:

WARFIELD, Berks
On 3rd February 1973, in 3 hours
5,001 SPLICED CATERS
In 100 methods with 288 changes of method

Anthony J. Cox	Treble	Anthony R. Peake	6
*Anita D. O'Brien	2	William Butler	7
Jennifer M. Taylor	3	John H. Fielden	8
James R. Taylor	4	Brian Bladon	9
Timothy G. Pett	5	D. John Hunt	Tenor

Composed and conducted by Anthony R. Peake
*First of Caters. First of Caters as conductor. First of Spliced Caters by all the band.

Most of the members of this band went on to ring peals in 110 Spliced Surprise Maximus, which were credited to the Gloucester and Bristol Diocesan Association.

In 1977 the following peal was rung for the Guild:

APPLETON, Oxon
On 17th December 1977, in 2 hours 57 minutes
5,040 SPLICED SURPRISE ROYAL
In 126 methods, 125 changes of method

Noel J. Diserens	Treble	Anthony R. Peake	6
Anita D. O'Brien	2	Bernard H. Taylor	7
Elisabeth A. G. Bowden	3	William Butler	8
Bernard F. L. Groves	4	Timothy G. Pett	9
Anthony J. Cox	5	John H. Fielden	Tenor
Composed by A. R. Peake		Conducted by T. G. Pett	

A Sunday Service band achieved a peal at Warfield in 1971 whilst the Bloxham band rang one at Rousham. In 1972 the local band at Hughenden rang a peal of Yorkshire for the 400th on the bells. Other anniversaries marked by peals were the Golden Jubilee of the first peals at Harwell and East Ilsley and the bicentenary of the first at East Hagbourne. In 1973 the 222nd anniversary of the first peal at High Wycombe was commemorated. Drayton recorded the 250th peal on the bells in 1971. The Banbury branch achieved a redoubtable peal in 1974 when their ringing master, Graham Clifton, conducted a peal which was not only his first, but also first for four other members of the band. The South Oxon branch mustered a band for the first time for a peal of Plain Bob Triples at Dorchester.

It became common for branches to organise quarter peals throughout their areas to mark anniversaries. The South Oxon did this for their Golden Jubilee and Banbury, and Witney and Woodstock did it for the Guild's ninetieth anniversary. The centenary of the East Berks and South Bucks branch was commemorated with peals at six towers, and that of the Sonning Deanery with peals at three towers. Quarter peals were rung as well. One peal and many quarters were rung by the North Bucks branch for their seventy-fifth anniversary in 1979.

Alan Pink scored his thousandth peal in April 1971. His name probably occurs more than any other in the Guild's list of first performances, mainly through the number of new methods he introduced and pealed for the first time. He was born at Ripley, Surrey on 5th December 1905, and learnt to handle a bell at Pulborough, Sussex. He moved into this diocese in 1932 when he obtained a job at Westminster Bank, Eton, and he soon began organising peals. He conducted peals in more than two dozen new Surprise methods in the years up to the War.

He served as a Naval officer during the War and managed to ring in South Africa and Australia. He arranged a peal at Sidney for naval personnel and locals and this move revitalised ringing in that area. After demobilisation he became Secretary to the Oxford Diocesan Board of Finance; in this capacity he met many incumbents and was able to use these contacts to arrange peals.

He was the thirty-ninth person to ring a thousand peals, achieving this milestone with a peal of Ashtead Surprise Major at Pulborough for the Sussex County Association. His total of 1,174, of which over 750 had been rung for the Guild, was remarkable considering he never rang two in a day, never went on a peal tour nor rang one on handbells. He helped many young ringers to score their first peal in a Surprise method. He had a severe heart attack in 1973, and was never really fit again; he died on 1st November 1980, aged 74.

Five more resident Guild members have scored one thousand peals. Bernard Groves moved to Reading in 1969 and was the thirty-fifth person to reach the target in March 1970, returning to his home county of Cheshire for the event. J. Alan Ainsworth has lived at Amersham since 1970, and was the forty-eighth to ring a thousand with a peal at Sunbury, for the Middlesex County Association in August 1974. The seventy-third person was Robert J. Crocker, who rang nearly five hundred peals for the Guild in six years. His thousandth was in November 1979 at St. Giles, Camberwell for the Ancient Society of College Youths.

Leonard Stilwell was born at Pulborough in 1890 and learnt to ring there in 1903. His first peal was Grandsire Triples in 1904; from 1906 to 1939 he lived in Windsor and rang many peals with Alan Pink's band. He returned to the diocese again in the 1960s and rang many more peals when he was in his late seventies! He rang his thousandth in 1975, nearly seventy-one years after his first!

WINDSOR, Berks
On 31st May 1975, in 3 hours
5,088 YORKSHIRE SURPRISE MAJOR

*Leonard Stilwell	Treble	A. Colin Banton	5
Alan R. Pink	2	Thomas J. Lock	6
Margaret Wenban	3	Derek E. Sibson	7
Edgar R. Rapley	4	Frank T. Blagrove	Tenor
Composed by R. Baldwin		Conducted by F. T. Blagrove	
*1,000th peal			

Leonard Stilwell is the oldest person to accomplish this feat. By contrast the youngest ever to achieve it, is David C. Brown who rang his at Aston Clinton for the Ancient Society of College Youths a few days after his twenty-fourth birthday. It took him just over ten years to ring them and in 1972 he rang the record number of 177!

A personal achievement of a different kind took place in 1972 when Frank C. Price rang two tower bells to peals of Cambridge Minor, Major, Royal, and Maximus for the Guild. In 1975 the Diserens family rang a peal of Plain Bob Major at Brightwell and the Butlers one on handbells in 1980.

Two long lengths were rung on tower bells and the first was of Belfast Surprise Major:

EAST TYTHERLEY, Hants

On 14th October 1972, in 6 hours 58 minutes

12,320 BELFAST SURPRISE MAJOR

Roger Baldwin	Treble	Brian Bladon	5
John R. Mayne	2	Bernard F. L. Groves	6
Maurice A. New	3	Timothy G. Pett	7
Brian J. Woodruffe	4	Noel J. Diserens	Tenor
Composed by S. Humphrey		Conducted by T. G. Pett _	

The longest length of Belfast yet rung.

The ringing of such a long length in this very difficult method calls for a high degree of concentration and endurance and ranks as a very considerable achievement.

The other peal was unusual in that it was the first long length ever to be rung by a ladies' band:

HUNGERFORD, Berks.

On 29th November, 1980, in 5 hours 57 minutes

10,080 EVESHAM SURPRISE MAJOR

Rebecca J. Dick	Treble	Geraldine R. Lea	5
Elizabeth A. Glasow	2	Sarah B. White	6
Anne L. Barter	3	Alison K. Surry	7
Elisabeth A. G. Bowden	4	Margaret Whiteley	Tenor

Composed by E. Shuttleworth. Conducted by R. J. Dick

The longest peal in the method

The highest number of peals yet rung for the Guild in a year was in 1976 when 280 were recorded. The next year was the occasion of the Queen's Silver Jubilee, and many were rung for this, although the final total was only 246.

*   *   *

One of the objects of the Guild is "the promotion of interest in the care of all the bells within the diocese." One means of doing this is by giving grants towards their repair and renovation. By 1971 the Restoration Fund, started in 1926, had built up to a sum of over £2,000. Grants were still small and, though welcome, did not offer a great deal of encouragement unless there was enthusiasm locally. In 1972 Henry Lawrenson discussed with the General Secretary an idea for floating a new fund with a very large capital sum, the interest from which would pay the whole cost for all the repairs in the diocese.

The scheme was fleshed out and presented to the Officers and Trustees at a meeting held in Drayton Vicarage on 15th January 1972. It was thought worth pursuing and Giles R. Sheddon, a Guild member and a practising solicitor, was asked to look over the proposals that had been tabled. He made some suggestions and on 11th March, a meeting of the Officers, Trustees and Stewards was held at Hughenden. They agreed to go ahead and asked Giles Sheddon to draft a constitution.

Another meeting on 21st August considered the draft, which was then submitted to the Charity Commissioners for their comments. It was introduced to the General Committee at their meeting in September and discussed again in March 1973. The scheme was then delayed for a year. After his election as Master in July 1973, Frederick Sharpe undertook to raise the matter with the Bishop of Oxford to enlist his personal support. The Bishop referred the matter to his Council, who deliberated upon it, and without knowing all the reasons for establishing such a fund, decided that the appeal should not have the official backing of the diocese.

The situation of cross-purposes continued, with the volumes of correspondence increasing by leaps and bounds. Eventually the Archdeacon of Oxford indicated that the Bishop was not opposed to the scheme in principle, but found himself in an embarrassing position as he was in the throes of launching a massive appeal to increase clergy stipends.

The scheme was put to the members at the Annual General Meeting at Kingham in July 1974 and received their approval. After that, the Rules were put to the General Committee on 21st September 1974 at Mapledurham and they were passed unanimously. The members of the General Committee are the Governors of the Oxford Diocesan Bell Fund, and they elect the Managing Trustees. The first people elected were: Frederick Sharpe, Chairman, William Butler, Secretary, Howard Oglesby, Treasurer, with Timothy G. Pett and Alan R. Pink as additional Trustees. The Custodian Trustees are Diocesan Trustees (Oxford) Ltd and the fund is registered with the Charity Commission under No. 268390.

Fund raising was launched in January 1975 and in the first year nearly £1,680 was raised. The £10,000 mark was passed in 1978 and it is hoped to have raised £25,000 by the end of the Centenary Year. The scheme only allows the interest to be used for grants and it will be many years before the intentions of the founders will be realised. In the foreseeable future, however, grants of 20% should be possible if applications are spread evenly. The chronicler of the second hundred years of the Guild's history may be able to report that all the bells of the diocese are ringable ... If he can, then our work has been well done.

POSTSCRIPT

In the preceding pages I have tried to indicate how the officers and members have carried out the aims and objectives of the Guild during the last century. The 1881 aims were:

1. To recognise the true position of ringers as church officers.
2. To cultivate the art of change ringing
3. To promote belfry reform where needed.

Long before the middle of the twentieth century belfry reform was completed and a new set of objects were outlined:

1. To encourage the attendance of members both at service ringing and at public worship.
2. The recruitment and training of ringers, so that there may be regular service ringing in all the towers in the diocese where the bells are ringable.
3. To cultivate the art of change ringing.
4. The promotion of interest in all the bells within the diocese.
5. To recognise the true position of ringers as church workers.

I think that we do meet these objectives. Events like the Festival and the services at branch meetings encourage the first. The second is covered by the work of the Education Committee, branch ringing masters, and tower captains. Change ringing has developed to a degree undreamt of by our forefathers. The Oxford Diocesan Bell Fund and the Towers and Belfries Committee stimulate interest in the bells in our towers, and lastly, more than ever before, ringers are involved in church work as choristers, sidesmens, churchwardens and lay readers.

Even so many ringers are apathetic towards the Guild and one or two splinter groups have formed peal-ringing societies. The liaison between the Guild and the University societies is not as close as it was in the past.

The Guild was a nineteenth century institution and we are now in the last quarter of the twentieth century. History shows that an organisation can never remain static; it either progresses or regresses. Fresh ideas must come forward and, despite opposition, changes will be made. As long as they are for the good of the Oxford Diocesan Guild of Church Bell Ringers, they should have the support of every single member.

APPENDIX I

GUILD OFFICERS 1881-1981

MASTER

Revd. F. E. Robinson	1881-1910
Revd. C. W. O. Jenkyn	1910-1933
Canon G. F. Coleridge	1933-1946
Canon C. E. Wigg	1946-1973
F. Sharpe	1973-1976
W. Butler	1976-

DEPUTY MASTER

Revd. C. W. O. Jenkyn	1905-1910
Canon C. E. Wigg	1933-1946
Capt. A. B. Poyntz	1946-1951
F. Sharpe	1951-1973
Dr. T. G. Pett	1973-1979
M. E. Dobson	1979-1981
R. A. Thorne	1981-

GENERAL SECRETARY

Revd. Dolben Paul	1881-1891
Revd. R. H. Hart-Davis	1891-1911
A. E. Reeves	1911-1917
R. T. Hibbert	1917-1945
W. Hibbert	1945-1956
Miss M. R. Cross	1956-1970
W. Butler	1970-1976
K. J. Darvill	1976-1981
M. E. Dobson	1981-

TREASURER

Revd. Dolben Paul	1881-1891
Revd. R. H. Hart-Davis	1891-1923
A. J. Wright	1923-1936
A. D. Barker	1936-1974
H. Oglesby	1974-1979
B. J. Gatward	1979-

APPENDIX II

VICE-PRESIDENTS

Revd. R. H. Hart Davis	1925	d. 1928
Revd. A. C. R. Freeborn	1926	d. 1930
W. Pole-Routh	1926	d. 1931
Canon G. F. Coleridge	1927	d. 1946
J. J. Parker	1927	d. 1937
Revd. T. Archer-Houblon	1929	d. 1932
Canon E. J. Norris	1933	d. 1940
J. Evans	1933	d. 1946
F. Sharpe	1949	d. 1976
Miss S. Davis	1951	d. 1960
T. J. Fowler	1954	d. 1959
T. Trollope	1956	d. 1960
E. Foster	1958	d. 1960
W. H. B. Wilkins	1958	d. 1962
Canon G. Dixon	1958	d. 1966
Rt. Revd. R. M. Hay	1960	d. 1973
A. D. Barker	1961	
O. S. Francis	1962	
W. G. Wilson	1963	
H. L. Roper	1964	
Mrs. G. E. Barker	1970	
Rt. Revd. D. G. Loveday	1971	
Miss M. R. Cross	1971	
Canon C. E. Wigg	1973	d. 1976
F. A. White	1979	
P. Walker	1980	
W. Butler	1981	

APPENDIX III

BIBLIOGRAPHY

Duckworth, Richard "Tintinnalogia" 1668 (1970 reprint)
Stedman, Fabian "Campanalogia" 1677
Morris, Ernest "History and Art of Change Ringing" 1931
Goldsmith, John S. "A Great Adventure" 1935
Cocks, Alfred H. "The Church Bells of Buckinghamshire" 1897
Robinson, Francis E. "Among the Bells" 1929
Trollope, J. Armiger "The College Youths" 1937
Sharpe, Frederick "The Church Bells of Oxfordshire" 1953
Sharpe, Frederick "The Church Bells of Berkshire" 1970
Church Bells
The Bell News
The Ringing World
Campanology
The Ringers' Magazine
Guild Reports
Minute books of the Guild
Minute books of the branches
Anthony Wood's Diaries
Thomas Hearne's Diaries
Peal book, Canon C. E. Wigg
Peal book, J. J. Parker
Peal book, R. T. Hibbert
Cuttings book, Revd. C. W. O. Jenkyn

APPENDIX IV

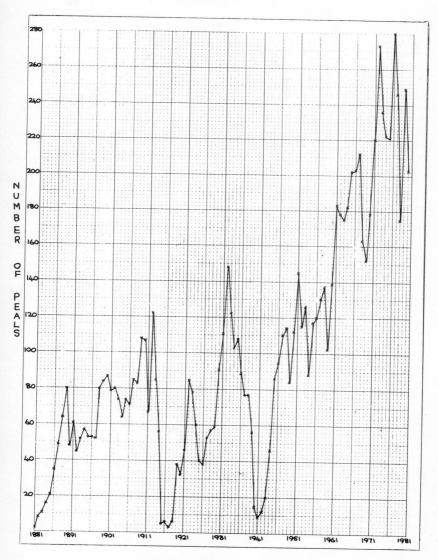

Analysis of Peals rung 1881-1980

LIST OF SUBSCRIBERS

R. F. M. Amies
Peter Anger
R. & L. E. Arnott

Brian M. Baldwin
Bampton Ringers
Arthur D. Barker
Gladys E. Barker
David K. Barrington
Noel C. Bartlett
Bedfordshire Association
Keith C. Begrie
Roland Biggs
Arthur Bird
William Birmingham
Hugh Bishop
Mary Bliss
Bradwell Abbey Field Centre
James Brooks
Phyllis Brown
John Butler
Buckinghamshire Library (12)

Cassington Tower
Chipping Norton Tower
Dawn Clarke
J. Clarke
Mavis Clarke (2)
Clavis Lodge No. 8585
G. J. Clifton
J. P. Coad
M. W. Coleman
David Cornwall
David J. Coveney
Peter R. Coveney
Brian Cox
Robert Crocker
David Cubitt

Michael A. R. Dane
Angela & Kenneth Darvill
Kenneth R. Davenport
Peter G. Davies
Mr. & Mrs. B. J. Davis
Noel J. Diserens
Mark E. Dobson
Donald H. A. Drayton

Clifford East
Easthampstead Tower
George Edmans
John C. Eisel
G. F. Elms
Edward J. Evans
Rosemary Evans
Eynsham Tower

Graham G. Firman
Katharine Firman
Elizabeth M. Fisher
Derek Fowles

Mr. & Mrs. B. J. Gatward (4)
David J. Gay
Frank Gibbard
Roy Goodwin
Ernest E. Gosling
Leslie J. Gregory
A. J. Griffin
E. M. Guiver

Haddenham Tower
John Harris
Roy T. Harris
Edward Hartley, M.B.E.
Andrew Hasledine
William H. Haynes
T. J. Hester
Arthur Hills
Barbara Hills
Robin J. Hine
B. Douglas Hird
Peter G. Holden
T. Geoffrey Holden
Mr. & Mrs. C. Holmes
Malcolm G. Hooton
Wilfred T. Huckin
Mark Hunter
Tony Hunter

W. Ivings

Anne E. Jones
Douglas Jordan
Peter Jordan
J. M. Joslin
David M. Joyce

F. Keen
Kidlington Tower (3)
Cyril H. Kinch
Charles J. Knight (2)

Heather Lamb
Henry Lawrenson
Walter Lee
Norman H. Leslie
Richard Lindars
Geoffrey Lindley
Linslade Tower (2)
Robert Lister
Margaret Lord

Ian A. Macgillivray
Jane Marlow
Richard J. Marshall
J. S. Mason
Bobbie May
G. McGregor
Ian M. Meyrick
William H. Mills
W. Mitchell

Mary M. Montgomery
Rosemary Morgan

Ruth M. Neller
M. Guy Nelson
David Nettel
A. Newton
P. Newton
Mr. & Mrs. R. P. Newton
D. A. Norris
J. A. Norris

J. N. O'Beirne
Christine I.Ottaway
Oxfordshire Library

Len Palfrey
Jennifer M. Parkinson
Judith Passant
E. D. Patching
Anthony R. Peake (2)
Edward J. Peett
Elizabeth M. Perks
Nigel Perrins
Martin Petchey
Hilarie Peters
Timothy G. Pett
Norman Phillips
Christopher J. Pickford
L. R. & M. S. Porter
Joan & Graham Prior
John Pusey

A. John Rance
L. C. & R. J. Renn
Dermot Roaf
David J. Rose
Tina Ruff
Geoffrey Runnicles

Jean Sanderson (3)
Stanley G. Scott
Dorothy Searing
William Simmonds
Neil O. Skelton
John M. Smeath
Mrs. A. D. Smith
Mr. & Mrs. H. Smith

Michael J. Smith
John A. Somers
John W. Spence
Derek Stainsby
Standlake Tower
Adrian Stanmore
John Starr
Mary E. Stone
Malcolm Story
Gwen Strong
E. George Swift (2)
Michael G. Swift

A. J. Thorne
Mr. & Mrs. R. A. Thorne
Susan Thornton
Basil Townsend
D. E. Towers
Geoffrey Tyler

T. & C. Wagstaff
E. Waite
Kenneth J. Wakefield
K. J. Wallace
Frank H. Walters
Sheila Watts
Mrs. M. Way
Frank West (2)
Lynne White
Winifred M. White
Florence E. Wigg
David C. Willis
Wilfrid G. Wilson
H. J. Wingrove
Witney Ringing Society
Witney & Woodstock Branch
Ven. C. Witton-Davies
Wokingham (All Saints)
Timothy A. Wooding
L.Roy Woodruff
Cyril A. Wratten

Edward R. Venn
Margaret Vince

Yarnton Tower
Mr. & Mrs. D. Young